ARTISTRY IN STONE:
GREAT STRUCTURES OF ANCIENT EGYPT

DON NARDO

LUCENT BOOKS

An imprint of Thomson Gale, a part of The Thomson Corporation

THOMSON
★
GALE

Detroit • New York • San Francisco • San Diego • New Haven, Conn. • Waterville, Maine • London • Munich

THOMSON
GALE

LIBRARY OF CONGRESS CATALOGING-IN-PUBLICATION DATA

Nardo, Don, 1947-
    Artistry in stone : great structures of ancient Egypt / by Don Nardo.
        p. cm. — (The Lucent library of historical eras)
    Includes bibliographical references and index.
    ISBN 1-59018-661-3 (hard cover : alk. paper)
    1. Egypt—Antiquities. 2. Monuments—Egypt. I. Title. II. Series: Lucent library of historical eras. Ancient Egypt.
    DT60.N3 2005
    932—dc22
                                                                    2004024455

Contents

Foreword

Looking back from the vantage point of the present, history can be viewed as a myriad of intertwining roads paved by human events. Some paths stand out—broad highways whose mileposts, even from a distance of centuries, are clear. The events that propelled the rise to power of Germany's Third Reich, its role in World War II, and its eventual demise, for example, are well defined and documented.

Other roads are less distinct, their route sometimes hidden from view. Modern legislatures may have developed from old tribal councils, for example, but the links between them are indistinct in places, open to discussion and interpretation.

The architecture of civilization—law, religion, art, science, and government—as well as the more everyday aspects of our culture—what we eat, what we wear—all developed along the historical roads and byways. In that progression can be traced every facet of modern life.

A broad look back along these roads reveals that many paths—though of vastly different character—seem to converge at a few critical junctions. These intersections are those great historical eras that echo over the long, steady course of human history, extending beyond the past and into the present.

These epic periods of time are the focus of Lucent's Library of Historical Eras. They shine through the mists of history like beacons, illuminated by a burst of creativity that propels events forward—so bright that we, from thousands of years away, can clearly see the chain of events leading to the present.

Each Lucent Library of Historical Eras consists of a set of books that highlight various aspects of these major eras. For example, the Elizabethan England library features volumes on Queen Elizabeth I and her court, Elizabethan theater, the great playwrights, and everyday life in Elizabethan London.

The mini-library approach allows for the division of each era into its most significant and most interesting parts and the exploration of those parts in depth. Also, social and cultural trends as well as illustrative documents and eyewitness accounts can be prominently featured in individual volumes.

Lucent's Library of Historical Eras presents a wealth of information to young readers. The lively narrative, fully documented primary and secondary source quotations, maps, photographs, sidebars, and annotated bibliographies serve as launching points for class discussion and further research.

In studying the great historical eras, students also develop a better understanding of our own times. What we learn from the past and how we apply it in the present may shape the future and may determine whether our era will be a guiding light to those traveling future roads.

THE LABOR OF FORGOTTEN MILLIONS

Modern visitors to Egypt are impressed by the widespread remains of large and imposing stone structures erected thousands of years ago. The most renowned of these are three "great" pyramids at Giza (near the modern capital, Cairo). The largest, commissioned by the pharaoh Khufu circa 2570 B.C., covers thirteen acres and originally towered to a height of 481 feet. It remained the tallest human-made structure in the world until the French built the Eiffel Tower in 1889.

In addition to this true architectural wonder (indeed, Khufu's pyramid was listed by the ancient Greeks as one of the seven wonders of their world), the countryside near the Nile River is dotted with other imposing ruins. These include the remains of other pyramids as well as temples, pylons (large ceremonial gateways), palaces, massive tombs, fortresses, and huge statues of rulers and gods. The remains of one temple complex (cluster of temples)—at

Karnak (on the east bank of the Nile near modern Luxor)—cover half a square mile. Awed by some of the buildings in the complex, in 1838 David Roberts, a gifted Scottish painter who captured many Egyptian ruins on canvas, remarked:

> You have to . . . walk among these gigantic structures to understand [their true immensity]. . . . The columns are over 30 feet in circumference, so that a man looks tiny beside them. The blocks that lie scattered all around are so huge that, even without considering how they were cut, it is impossible to imagine how they were brought here and put in their places.[1]

Marshaling the Masses

The creation of large-scale buildings was not unique to ancient Egypt, nor, of course, to the ancient world. Today, huge structures, including skyscrapers and sports stadiums, are commonplace. Thanks to giant cranes, trucks, tractors, elevators, welding tools, steel girders, and other modern construction devices and tools, an enormous building can be erected in months or a year or two at most. And advanced technology allows such projects to be completed by relatively few people. While a few hundred individuals who specialize in the building trades are putting up a new office building, for example, tens of millions of their fellow citizens are engaged in other trades or pursuits.

The great buildings of ancient Egypt were created under markedly different circumstances. And it is often difficult for travelers to modern Egypt to gain a true appreciation for the tremendous amount of human labor needed to erect them. The Egyptians had no machines. Every step of construction had to be accomplished using the simplest of tools, driven or aided by the brute force of muscle power.

Moreover, the workforce, including laborers, artisans, and various support personnel, made up a significant proportion of

This nineteenth-century Scottish artist David Roberts painted this atomospheric view of the great temple at Abu Simbel.

society as a whole. These masses, constituting a veritable army, had to be marshaled and directed by the government in what amounted to a major national effort. Dieter Arnold, a leading authority on ancient Egyptian building methods, elaborates:

> A considerable part of the population of Egypt, either directly or indirectly, was continually occupied in building projects all over the country. The erection of the pyramids [at Giza] and the gigantic temples of [the pharaohs] Amenhotep III and Ramesses II [at Karnak and elsewhere] are only the most eminent peaks of this activity. Hundreds of thousands of cubic meters of limestone and sandstone, alabaster, granite and basalt were quarried from the cliffs along the Nile Valley and the surrounding deserts. Hundreds of boatloads of timber had to be imported from [foreign lands]. Large quantities of tools and other equipment had to be produced. . . . Mountains of sand and Nile mud had to be moved for the fabrication of brick. Finally, all this vast amount of material had to be brought to the construction site and lifted into position.

The huge temple complex at Karnak required the labor of tens of thousands of workers over the course of several generations.

This reenactment of a large-scale building project in ancient Egypt was staged for the 1956 film version of The Ten Commandments.

For this purpose, thousands of people had to be conscripted [by government officials] according to complicated procedures, and steered to the many building projects. These people had to be trained, fed, and clothed. The gigantic apparatus [of the country's construction industries] was masterminded and then enforced by the pharaoh with his priests and officials.[2]

Traditional Views of the Workers

Who were these workers who erected Egypt's great monuments? And how do modern scholars know about them and how they accomplished these impressive feats? In general, the evidence for the ancient Egyptian builders and their works comes from two sources. The first consists of the surviving accounts of Greek and Roman writers who visited or lived in Egypt in the last few centuries B.C. and first few centuries A.D. (In those centuries, after conquest first by Greeks and then by Romans, Egypt was no longer an independent nation.) The second major source consists of studies of the ruins of the buildings themselves, supplemented by ongoing discoveries made by archaeologists. Each year, their digs reveal new information about the workers' tools, construction methods, dwellings, personal items, social customs, and so forth.

Regarding the surviving accounts of ancient writers, one that early modern scholars studied and in many cases accepted as accurate was that of the fifth-century B.C. Greek historian Herodotus. He took a long tour of Egypt and interviewed many locals, including some who professed to be priests. (In ancient Egypt, priests were among the most educated and respected members of society.) In his *Histories*, Herodotus later claimed that Khufu, whom he called Cheops, was an oppressive ruler who forced many of his subjects to work as slaves on massive building projects, including the Great Pyramid. He "compelled his subjects without exception to labor as slaves for his own advantage," the historian said.

> Some were forced to drag blocks of stone from the quarries . . . to the Nile, where they were ferried across and taken over by others. . . . The work went on in three monthly shifts, a hundred thousand men in a shift. It took ten years of this oppressive slave labor to build the track along which the blocks were hauled. . . . To build the pyramid itself took twenty years.[3]

This image of thousands of slaves toiling to build the pyramids and other Egyptian monuments was widely accepted for nearly twenty-four centuries. However, Herodotus turned out to be wrong. He visited Egypt more than two thousand years after the Giza pyramids were constructed; and by that time the builders and construction methods had been long forgotten. Most of what the Greek historian's guides and interviewees knew about the pyramids consisted of tall tales, which they undoubtedly believed and dutifully passed along to him.

Incentives for Working in Construction

Modern scholarship has revealed the truth about the pyramid builders, namely that most were ordinary folk, mainly rural farmers (but also some craftsmen and laborers from the larger towns). The farmers' lives were regulated in large degree by natural cycles, especially the annual flooding of the Nile River. Each year, usually like clockwork, the river gently overflowed its banks and drenched farmers' fields with the freshwater needed to ensure healthy harvests. During the months of the flood season it was not possible to work the land, and most farmers had at least some free time on their hands. Many of them filled that time by laboring on government-sponsored projects, including the building of pyramids, temples, and other large stone structures. Recent evidence suggests that some construction projects continued into other seasons. If so, the government called on an unknown number of peasants to leave their fields and work for the king.

Assuming they were not forced at sword point (and no evidence exists that they were), what motivated large numbers of farmers to become part-time construction workers, either during or after the flood season? First, a good deal of evidence suggests that performing such work fulfilled certain tax obligations. So there was a practical incentive for the workers. As explained in a recent popular study of the building of the pyramids:

> Conscripted labor—some modern accounts call it "corvée" labor, a kind of tax paid with work rather than goods—was the essential fuel of every major construction project [in ancient Egypt]. Roads, canals, mines, public monuments—all were dug or built by conscripts. . . . The practice of corvée labor was so firmly established in the Egyptian scheme of things that . . . important people were buried with miniature figurines, intended to take on any corvée labor that might be demanded of the dead person by the gods. [4]

The Richest God in History

Amun-Ra, to whom much of the great complex of temples at Karnak was dedicated, became the central god of the New Kingdom. This description of the god is by noted Near Eastern scholar Desmond Stewart (from his book on the pyramids and the Sphinx).

Amun had long been the local god of Thebes. . . . The meaning of Amun was "hidden," and thanks to the instinctive process whereby the Egyptians sought for the one behind the many, he became regarded as the invisible force of the Sun, and therefore truly universal. His name was linked with Ra, the chief deity of the pyramid builders [i.e., rulers of the Old Kingdom]. Sculpted as a radiantly handsome man in a high-plumed headdress, he became the chief god of imperial [New Kingdom] Egypt. . . . Many surviving prayers testify that he answered the appeals of the poor as swiftly as those of the strong. But in a worldly sense, as the proprietor of the world's largest temple, Amun-Ra was the richest god in history.

This nineteenth-century painting was based on ancient depictions of the god Amun-Ra.

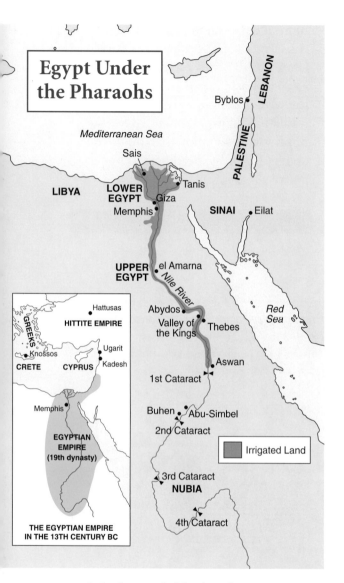

Egypt Under the Pharaohs

Mediterranean Sea

LEBANON

Byblos

PALESTINE

Sais

LOWER EGYPT

Tanis

LIBYA

Giza

Memphis

SINAI

Eilat

UPPER EGYPT

el Amarna

Nile River

Red Sea

GREEKS

Hattusas

HITTITE EMPIRE

Abydos

Valley of the Kings

Thebes

Ugarit

Knossos

CRETE

CYPRUS

Kadesh

Aswan

1st Cataract

Memphis

Buhen

Abu-Simbel

2nd Cataract

EGYPTIAN EMPIRE (19th dynasty)

Irrigated Land

3rd Cataract

NUBIA

THE EGYPTIAN EMPIRE IN THE 13TH CENTURY BC

4th Cataract

favorably on a worker. As one scholar suggests, "Helping to build a residence for the king to reign in for all eternity meant securing a share of immortality for oneself." [5]

A Memorial to Sweat and Blood

Thus, thousands of imposing monuments erected in ancient Egypt over the course of some three thousand years were the result of the accumulated labor of millions of everyday Egyptians. The names of most of these workers have not survived. Indeed, the vast majority were never recorded in the first place. This is because ancient historians and scribes almost always focused on the personalities, lives, and deeds of famous, wealthy, and powerful people. We know, therefore, that the so-called Great Pyramid at Giza was erected as the final resting place for a pharaoh named Khufu. But all but a few of the multitudes who labored for years to make that enduring monument a reality have been long forgotten, at least as individuals. (The "few" in this case are those whose small tombs were discovered near Khufu's pyramids during the 1990s.)

In a strange twist of fate, a memorial to the collective existence of all the workers who worked for Khufu has survived in the form of the pyramid itself. For all eternity they will share the credit for it with the pharaoh. After all, without their sweat and blood, it and Egypt's many other impressive stone structures could never have been built.

It is also probable that there was a spiritual incentive as well. In the period in which the great pyramids were erected, the Egyptian peasants believed that their pharaoh was a god, or at least that he was blessed and guided by the gods. To take part in the building of a monument that glorified him was therefore an honor and would hopefully make the gods look

Chapter One

PYRAMIDS: CUTTING, LIFTING, AND SETTING THE STONES

R oyal tombs shaped like pyramids are the most famous, as well as the largest, of the many great stone monuments erected by the ancient Egyptians. The vast majority of Egypt's pyramids were built in a roughly nine-century span beginning just after 2700 B.C. and ending shortly after 1800 B.C. The better part of these centuries encompassed the Old and Middle Kingdoms, two of the three major eras into which modern scholars divide ancient Egyptian history. By the advent of the third great age—the New Kingdom, which lasted from about 1550 to 1069 B.C.—pyramids were no longer built. (There were several other eras before, between, and after the big three, including the last two, in which first Greeks and then Romans ruled Egypt.)

In fact, by the beginning of the New Kingdom, the largest and most famous pyramids—those on the Giza plateau—were relics a thousand years old. Their inner tombs had long ago been looted of their valuables. And the nearby quarries and workers' villages used in their construction had been buried by sand and debris and forgotten. At least the New Kingdom Egyptians remembered who had erected these giant monuments, namely the pharaohs Khufu, Khafre, and Menkaure. Historians now know that their truly enormous pyramids were created in a period of only about seventy-five years (ca. 2585–ca. 2510 B.C.). All three rulers belonged to Egypt's Fourth Dynasty. (A dynasty is a family line of rulers.)

Though the kings of the Fourth Dynasty built the most impressive pyramids, they did not invent the pyramidal tomb. This architectural form developed gradually from smaller tombs constructed for members of the upper classes beginning centuries before the Old Kingdom. These were flat-topped, rectangular structures called mastabas (from an Egyptian word meaning "bench," because they looked much like simple wooden benches). The mastabas had a serious drawback. They were made of mud bricks, which disintegrated rapidly, rendering such tombs considerably less permanent than their builders would have liked. Mud-brick structures were also easy for tomb robbers to break into.

Seeking more permanence and security, builders made these structures larger and switched to using stone, which is far less susceptible to erosion by the elements.

King Djoser's pyramid at Sakkara. The inset shows the closely fitted stones of a wall at the structure's base.

A milestone was the tomb of the second pharaoh of the Old Kingdom—Djoser. The original plan was for a large stone mastaba. But the architect, Imhotep, eventually came up with the ingenious idea of stacking six stone mastabas on top of one another, each slightly smaller than the one below, thereby creating the world's first pyramid (today called the Step Pyramid).

Other pharaohs erected step pyramids. Then they began filling in the notches of the steps, producing the first smooth-sided versions. By the start of the Fourth Dynasty (ca. 2686 B.C.), building such pyramids was the rage, and the first ruler of that dynasty, Sneferu, erected several. As history has shown, his son, Khufu, and grandson, Khafre, greatly outdid him.

It is not merely the great size of these monuments that continues to astonish people to this day. Rather, it is the fact that they were built using very rudimentary tools and construction methods. Indeed, the pyramid builders lacked even the basic block and tackle (made of pulleys and ropes), which the later Greeks and Romans took for granted, and relied mainly on simple levers and raw muscle power, aided by dogged persistence.

Quarrying the Stones

Examining the various steps involved in building the Giza pyramids does more than demonstrate the patience, perseverance, and ingenuity of the builders. It also reveals, for the most part, how ancient Egyptian builders worked in general. This is because the majority of the materials,

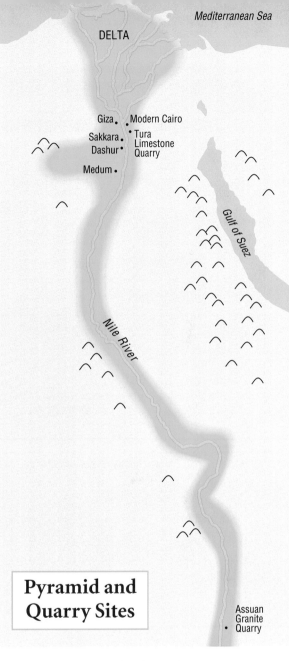

tools, quarrying methods, and transporting and lifting techniques used to raise the pyramids were also employed in building temples, fortresses, and many other monumental (large-scale) structures.

Quarrying the stones is a case in point. The most common general types of stone

Designer of the First Pyramid

In his book about Egyptian myths, University of London scholar George Hart gives this short sketch of Imhotep, who was the architect of the first pyramid (the Step Pyramid of Djoser) and was later worshipped as a god.

A limestone bust from a lost statue of King Djoser . . . preserves the name and titles of Imhotep: "Seal-bearer of the King of Lower Egypt, one who is near the head of the King [i.e., vizier], director of the Great Mansion, Royal representative, High Priest of Heliopolis, Imhotep, the carpenter and sculptor." . . . In addition to [Djoser's] pyramid complex, Imhotep was the architect of a sanctuary to the Sun god at Heliopolis,

dedicated by Djoser and surviving today only in fragments. . . . His reputation as an experienced architect led to his adoption by the scribes of Egypt as the most eminent practitioner of their craft. He became regarded as a source of intellectual inspiration and a number of moral maxims were alleged to have been committed to papyrus in his name. . . . At some point . . . his role as a sage became enhanced by attributing his birth to the direct intervention of one of the major gods. Imhotep became "son of Ptah," creator god of Memphis. . . . His [Imhotep's] main temple was in North Sakkara, with a subsidiary sanctuary in Memphis, southwest of the main temple of Ptah.

used in building projects in Egypt were limestone and sandstone. And the Giza pyramids were made mostly of limestone. (Much smaller amounts of harder granite were used to line the inner tomb chambers.) The softer varieties of limestone and sandstone (such as red sandstone) could be cut relatively easily using metal chisels, saws, and drills. (At first, copper was the chief metal used. Bronze, an alloy of copper and tin, was introduced during the Middle Kingdom and became very widespread in the New Kingdom, while much harder and more reliable iron tools did not become common in Egypt until the Roman period, which began in 30 B.C.) In contrast, harder varieties of limestone and sandstone, along with harder stones like gran-

ite and basalt, could be cut or crushed only using hammers and picks made of even harder stone.

The bulk of the limestone used to make Khufu's pyramid came from a quarry located right on the Giza plateau, less than half a mile from the pyramid. This was an open quarry, as opposed to a covered or closed quarry in which the workers must tunnel into a mountain or cliff to reach the desired stone. (Both types were exploited in ancient Egypt.)

Throughout most of ancient times, the general method the Egyptians used in an open quarry was to outline the shape of the blocks and then cut them out of the stone. The first step was to use paint or chisel marks to create a grid of large rectangles on a wide, flat stone surface in the quarry. The marking was done in such a way that the outlines of the blocks were separated from one another by about a foot. The workers used cutting and pounding tools to turn these areas of separation into narrow trenches, so that the sides of the trenches became the sides of the emerging blocks. Kate Spence, a specialist in ancient Egyptian building techniques, describes the final steps: "The trenches were cut a little below the intended depth of the block, which was then slightly undercut, split from its bed using wooden levers, and dragged out from the front."[6] (Another method was to chisel grooves in the stone, insert wooden wedges, soak the wedges with water, and wait until the wedges swelled and cracked the stone. It does not seem to have been introduced until shortly before the beginning of the Greek period, which lasted from 323 to 30 B.C.)

Dressing the Stones

Having separated a stone block from the quarry, the workers used wooden levers and muscle power to load it onto a wooden sledge (which resembled a large sled). Then they attached ropes to the sledge and dragged it away. The stone blocks emerging from the quarry were divided into two general groups. The first, and by far the largest, group consisted of those stones that would be used for foundations or core (interior) sections of the pyramid. It did not matter if the texture of their outer faces was rough (as all the surfaces were when first quarried), so these needed no dressing (smoothing or refining). Some were hauled right to the construction site, but others were deposited in a holding area to be used when needed.

In contrast, many of the stone blocks in the outer layers of the structure needed to fit more precisely so that their outer surfaces would appear as uniform and smooth as possible. (In the case of pyramids, these blocks had to fit flush with polished casing stones added in the final stage; in structures like temples, the outer stones had to be dressed because they were directly visible and often bore paintings and sculpted scenes.) To this end, workers dressed the bottom face and at least one side face of such a block. To trim excesses, they employed copper or bronze saws and chisels. Then they used a piece of sandstone to grind down smaller irregularities.

During the final stages of dressing a stone, workers often needed to test and correct the flatness of its surface. Dieter Arnold describes the clever ways they did this:

To test the flatness of the surface, it could be touched with a . . . wooden board covered with red paint. The color would stick to the protruding areas, which then had to be treated again. . . . Another tool, which probably was more frequently used, was the boning rod. Two equally long rods were connected at their tops by a string that could thus be stretched [with the rods held vertically] over the surface to be tested. A third rod of the same length [also held vertically] could be held under the string [and run back and forth over the stone's surface. . . . If there still [were] protruding parts, the third rod would show above the line of the string [and a mason would use a hammer and chisel to chop off the protruding parts].[7]

Leveling the Base

Before the undressed and dressed stones could be laid down in courses (layers), thereby assembling the pyramid, the builders had to make sure the base, or foundation, of the structure was as level as possible. Otherwise, its enormous overall weight would not be evenly distributed; this could make it unstable and more prone to cracking and crumbling.

The builders of Khufu's pyramid achieved an amazing degree of accuracy in leveling its base. The variation in flatness from one end of the enormous structure to the other is only about three-quarters

In this modern drawing, workers dress stone blocks (center, background) while others drag dressed blocks to their preset places.

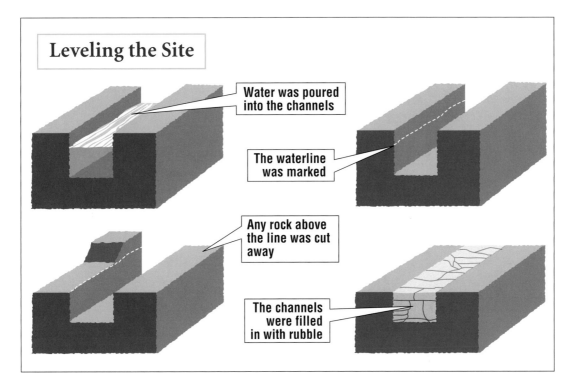

Leveling the Site

Water was poured into the channels

The waterline was marked

Any rock above the line was cut away

The channels were filled in with rubble

of an inch. A number of theories have been proposed to explain how this feat was accomplished. The most widely accepted until recently involved using water as a leveling tool. In this scheme, workers dug trenches around the site and flooded the area with water. Because standing water is always perfectly level, marks made at its surface along the edges of the site would all be at the same height; and after draining the water, these marks would become guides for laying the foundation stones.

Although some scholars still accept this theory, others now think it would have been too difficult for the workers to create an artificial lake atop the Giza plateau. They suggest instead a scenario supported by the existence of lines of small holes still visible near the outer edges of Khufu's and Khafre's pyramids. "The likely explanation," say researchers Kevin Jackson and Jonathan Stamp,

is that [the holes] were used to hold stakes with a long cord strung along them which could be used in conjunction with [an] ordinary plumb-line [a rod from which a weight hung on a string, creating a vertical line] to establish exact heights and then be conveniently removed when the builders needed to move in a new stone. Using these guidelines . . . the builders were able to achieve exceptional precision by carefully adjusting the level of the pyramid's foundation platform, not that of the raw bedrock on which it rested. [8]

This scene from the 1955 film Land of the Pharaohs *depicts the use of a brick ramp to raise the stones of Khufu's pyramid.*

Raising the Stones

Once the foundation stones of a pyramid were laid, workers could begin stacking the stones in courses. For the first few courses, this was not particularly difficult, as the sledges bearing the stones could be pulled up short timber ramps running from the ground to the top of a course. As the courses rose higher, however, the job became increasingly arduous. The average stone block used in Khufu's pyramid weighed about two and a half tons. (Some stones used in the structure's interior were considerably heavier.) And to carry such loads to the higher courses, wooden ramps would have needed to be so long, thick, and heavy that they would have been impractical to build and move.

To overcome this problem, the builders used ramps made by piling up large mounds of sand mixed with small pieces of limestone and other stone debris. After the last courses of stone were in place, the ramps were removed. It is reasonable to ask where all of this excess material ended up. Modern archaeologists found a great deal of it in the excavated sections of Khufu's quarry at Giza; and most scholars now think that the builders purposely dumped it there. (In so doing, they initiated the process by which the quarry was buried and forgotten.)

The burning question for modern investigators has long been: How were these ramps shaped? There is no clear-cut answer because at least seven or eight workable configurations are possible. Moreover, some evidence suggests that there was no standard approach or method. Instead, it is quite probable that differently shaped debris ramps were used for different pyramids. In fact, some scholars have proposed that two or more different configurations might have been used for Khufu's pyramid alone, depending on the stage of the work and the specific needs to be met.

Among the likely ramp configurations used for Khufu's pyramid is a single linear, or straight-on, version constructed at a right angle to one side of the structure. This would have been logical and useful for the lower third or maybe lower half of the courses. However, to reach the courses above these, such a ramp would need to be so tall and long that building it would be, in Jackson and Stamp's words, "a tremendous drain on manpower."[9]

Other possible ramps that may have supplemented the linear one include a spiral version running around three or all four sides of the pyramid; a reversing, or zigzag, version running back and forth along one side; and multiple small linear ramps on all four sides. Kate Spence favors the latter approach for the bulk of the work because of its practical utility. "Approximately 96 percent of the volume of a pyramid is in its bottom two-thirds," she points out. "And during construction of the lower courses, many small ramps may have ensured a high flow rate of blocks to the working levels." However, she cautions that "it seems likely that different solutions for raising blocks were used as the project progressed."[10] At present, no firm scholarly consensus has emerged about exactly which kinds of ramps were used in constructing the Giza pyramids.

The Finishing Touches

Whatever the shape of the ramps, with their aid the workers eventually set all of the stone blocks in their courses. At that

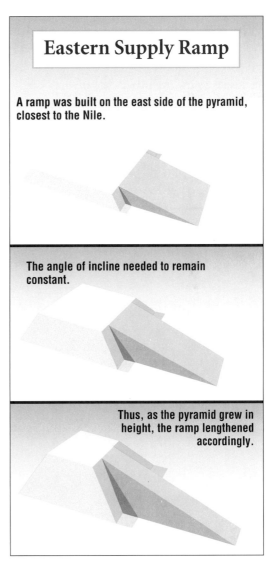

Eastern Supply Ramp

A ramp was built on the east side of the pyramid, closest to the Nile.

The angle of incline needed to remain constant.

Thus, as the pyramid grew in height, the ramp lengthened accordingly.

point, Khufu's pyramid looked more or less like it does today (minus the cracks, chips, weathering, and discoloration accumulated over the centuries). However, the structure was not complete until a layer of casing stones was added. (In medieval and early modern times, scavengers stripped off most of these stones for use in smaller building projects.) The casing stones for the Giza pyramids did not come from the local quarry because the builders felt its limestone was not fine and white enough. So they imported it from a quarry at Tura, located a few miles away on the other side of the Nile.

Unlike the regular blocks making up the pyramid, the casing stones were not shaped like rectangles. Instead, the casing blocks were square in the back and slanted at an angle in the front. The square back part of such a stone filled the notch, or step, that existed where one course of rectangular blocks was indented from the one below it. (In other words, the bottom of the casing stone rested on the step, and the back of the casing stone fit flush against the face of the next course of rectangular blocks.) The slanted outer edges, or faces, of the casing stones merged to create a solid, flat, polished, highly attractive outer surface for the structure.

The finished Giza pyramids were not merely beautiful. Indeed, their sheer enormity made them imposing, impressive, even awe inspiring. Khufu's, which bore the

The pyramids of Khufu, Khafre, and Menkaure dominate the landscape south of Cairo. In ancient times, Khufu's tomb stood 481 feet high.

Egyptian construction workers were organized into gangs. This scene from Land of the Pharaohs *shows one such gang dragging a large stone block.*

name Akhet-Khufu ("Khufu's Horizon"), towered to a height of 481 feet, measured 756 feet on each side, and covered more than thirteen acres of ground. (Today, it is only 451 feet high, mainly because its upper casing stones are missing.) In all, approximately 2.3 million limestone blocks were used in its construction. Though smaller than Khufu's pyramid, the other two Giza giants were architectural marvels in their own right, as Khafre's tomb stood 478 feet high and Menkaure's 220 feet. These structures were so tall and massive that they were visible from a distance of many miles.

How Many Workers?

Considering the simplistic methods employed to quarry, transport, lift, and assemble the stones, building these amazing monuments was a very labor-intensive operation. It required a long time and many workers. But how long and how many? Among the major questions Egyptologists have long addressed are the size of the labor force for such a project, how these workers were organized, how long it took a set number of laborers to accomplish certain tasks, and where the workers lived while raising the monuments.

It has been established that the pyramids were not built by slaves, as the Greek historian Herodotus claimed. Rather, these magnificent monuments were built by free laborers, mostly small farmers working for the government during the Nile flood season. From studying documents, graffiti (carved onto the sides of pyramids and other structures), and other ancient sources, scholars know that these laborers were organized into various-sized groups, or gangs.

The largest known gang was two thousand strong and broke down into two units of one thousand men each. Graffiti from Menkaure's pyramid attests that the members of one of the thousand-man units who worked on the structure proudly called themselves the Friends of Menkaure. Another group was known as the Drunkards of Menkaure. Such a group further broke down into five two-hundred-man groups, called *zaa* by the Egyptians and *phyles* (meaning "tribes") by the Greeks. The *zaa* had names such as "Green," "Little," "Asiatic," and "Great." Each of these two-hundred-man groups further broke down into units of ten to twenty workers each. "Life," "Perfection," and "Endurance" are among the known names used by these smallest workers' groups.

The number of these groups needed to build a pyramid the size of Khufu's or Khafre's would naturally depend to some degree on how long the project took to complete. Herodotus claimed it took twenty years. There is no way to tell if this figure is too high, too low, or just about right.

Assuming Herodotus was about right, it does not follow that his estimate of one hundred thousand workers was also correct. In fact, most scholars now feel that the actual workforce was much smaller. Some of the strongest evidence for this was provided by Harvard University scholar Mark Lehner, one of the world's leading Egyptologists. In the 1990s he conducted a unique experiment in conjunction with the television science program *Nova*. Under his supervision, a gang of twelve men recreated the typical daily labors of the pyramid workers (going so far as to go barefoot and live in primitive shelters in the desert). In twenty-one days, they managed to quarry 186 stone blocks the same size and weight as those in the Giza pyramids. From this and other experiments, which involved dragging and setting the stones, Lehner calculated that five thousand or fewer workers could have built Khufu's pyramid in twenty years. (It follows, then, that ten thousand workers could have done it in ten years.)

Workers' Villages and Cemeteries

Five or ten thousand laborers certainly does not sound like an inordinately large number to raise a monument as large as Khufu's pyramid in the course of a generation. But this number can be misleading. It must be kept in mind that it took more than just quarrymen, draggers, and stone setters—what might be called the core laborers—to build such structures. Large numbers of backup workers were needed to support and sustain the core laborers. According to Jackson and Stamp, these backup workers included:

carpenters to make the "railways" and sleds [on which many of the stones were dragged], water carriers to keep them slick, potters to make those water vessels, toolmakers to keep up a steady

Bakeries to Feed the Workers

The workers' settlement discovered on the Giza plateau featured some well equipped bakeries, described here by noted Egyptian archaeologist Zahi Hawass in a January 1997 article for Archaeology *magazine.*

Each bakery was about 17 feet long and eight feet wide. Inside each room lay a pile of broken bread pots discarded after the last batch of bread was removed 4,600 years ago. Though Egyptian written records attest at least 14 types of bread, we found only small and large bell-shaped pots and flat trays. Along the east wall were two lines of holes in a shallow trench, resembling an egg carton. The holes had held dough-filled pots while hot coals and ash in the trench baked the bread. A hearth in the southeastern corner would have been used to heat pots before they were inverted as lids on dough-filled containers in the trench.

A painting found in a tomb near Thebes shows bakers working at a construction site.

supply of replacements and repairs, overseers to make sure the work was done efficiently, and scribes—many, many scribes—to keep a steady tally of what was being done and where. And, of course, an army marches on its stomach. There would need to be a corps of cooks and bakers and butchers and brewers; additional builders to construct the ovens in which they cooked, as well as the barracks in which the basic workforce was quartered.[11]

In all—counting core laborers, backup workers, and their families—modern esti-

The remains of mastabas and other smaller tombs dot the landscape near Khafre's massive pyramid-tomb.

mates of the total labor force range from twenty to forty thousand.

Where were these workers housed while building Khufu's pyramid (as well as the other pyramids at Giza)? For a long time no one could be sure. But in the 1990s Lehner and Zahi Hawass, Egypt's leading archaeologist, began excavating an ancient workers' village located right on the Giza plateau near the pyramids and dating from the time of their construction. Hawass later wrote:

> During the construction of the sewage system [near] the great pyramid, we found a large Old Kingdom settlement about 3 km [1.8 miles] square. We recorded a continuous layer of mud-brick buildings.... Among the artifacts [excavated] are thousands of fragments of every day pottery and bread molds, cooking pots, beer jars, and trays for sifting grain and flour ... [as well as] domesticated animal bones, such as beef, pork and sheep with butchers marks on them.... I believe that there were two types of settlement, one for the workmen who moved the stones, and the other camp for the artisans [who dressed the stones].... We [also] found the tombs of the workmen who built the pyramids. [12]

These tombs, which form a sprawling cemetery, are much smaller and more humble than the royal pyramid tombs that loom nearby. Most consist of pits dug in the sand, often lined with mud bricks, and topped by two-to-six-foot stone caps. The cemetery features more than six hundred

of these, which probably belonged to average laborers. About thirty slightly larger and more elaborate tombs found in the cemetery were likely the final resting places of overseers, who occupied a slightly higher place on the social ladder.

Various artifacts discovered in these tombs reveal tantalizing facts about the lives and habits of the workers who raised the nearby pyramids. As Hawass explains:

> The tombs come in a variety of forms: stepped domes, beehives, and gabled roofs. Two to six feet high, the domes covered simple rectangular grave pits, following the configuration of the pyramids in an extremely simplified form. One small tomb featured a miniature ramp leading up and around its dome. Could the builder have intended it to represent the construction ramp of a royal pyramid? ... We have found many false doors and stelae [stone markers] attached to these tombs.... Inscribed in crude hieroglyphs, they record the names of the people whose skeletons lay below.... Small stone figurines in a rectangular niche ... represent [the members of] a household of these workers. One of the statuettes depicts a woman seated on a backless chair with her hands on her knees.... She wears a black wig with hair parted in the middle and reaching to her shoulders.... Study of the [skeletal] remains [of those buried in the cemetery] ... reveals that males and females were equally represented, mostly buried in fetal positions, with face to the east

and head to the north. Many of the men died between the ages of 30 and 35. Below the age of 30, a higher mortality was found in females ... undoubtedly reflecting the hazards of childbirth. [13]

A Proud Legacy

Thus, thanks to dedicated archaeologists like Lehner and Hawass, some of the workers who toiled to raise one of the wonders of the ancient world are no longer nameless and forgotten. They have emerged as flesh-and-blood individuals who laughed, cried, baked bread, married, had children, devoutly worshipped the gods, and respected the memory of their fallen kin and friends by erecting modest tombs for them.

Still, history will always remember these workers for the larger tombs they created—those of pharaohs. It was an accomplishment that was seldom equaled in the annals of human history. To have one's work survive and continue to inspire new generations for thousands of years is a legacy that undoubtedly would have made both the pharaohs and the workers beam with pride.

Chapter Two

Pyramids: Chambers, Security, and Mystical Elements

Though impressive and fascinating in their own right, the outer facades of the Giza pyramids and the construction methods used to create them represent only part of the story of these awesome monuments. The design and execution of their interiors, as well as the way they were aligned on the Giza plateau, had crucial religious significance and were carefully thought out in advance. Even the basic shape of these structures was chosen because it had religious and mystical meaning.

This fusion (mixture or blending) of architecture and physical construction with religious beliefs and symbolism comes as no surprise. On the one hand, the Egyptians were extremely devout reli-

giously. Herodotus said that "they are religious to excess, beyond any other nation in the world." [14] Indeed, religious observance and symbolism permeated all levels of ancient Egyptian society, including political, personal, and artistic expression.

Therefore, the pyramids were not simply big mounds of stone designed to show off the pharaoh's power and prestige (although this was certainly one of their functions). First and foremost, a pyramid was a pharaoh's tomb. Because the pharaoh was seen as a semidivine being, his welfare, including his existence in the afterlife, was tied directly to the welfare of the country and its people as a whole. Accordingly, all aspects of the tomb's creation had to be as correct as possible in order to ensure that

Passageways for the Soul?

Two narrow shafts run out of the King's Chamber in Khufu's pyramid. Too small for a human being to walk or even crawl through, they have long puzzled modern scholars. One theory was that they were air vents to bring fresh air into the central chamber. But they may have served an additional function, as explained by Kevin Jackson and Jonathan Stamp in this excerpt from their book Building the Great Pyramid.

In the north and south walls [of the King's Chamber], about 3 feet from the floor, are single apertures [openings]. The northern one is the opening for a long, narrow shaft which runs all the way up to the pyramid's exterior face at an angle of thirty-one degrees. The southern one runs in the same way, at an angle of 45 degrees. . . . The northern shaft is oriented toward the North Pole star; the southern shaft to the constellation of Orion. . . . For the Egyptians, a royal tomb was much more than a place where remains were kept. It was the king's gateway to the stars—a launch-pad to the afterlife. . . . And this is almost certainly the explanation of those intriguing narrow passages cut from the King's Chamber. . . . In both literal and figurative terms, they are the channels up which [the soul of] Khufu would pass to . . . be set among the stars.

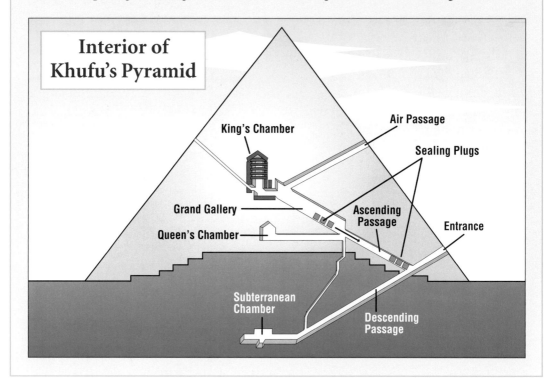

Interior of Khufu's Pyramid

King's Chamber · Air Passage · Sealing Plugs · Grand Gallery · Ascending Passage · Queen's Chamber · Entrance · Subterranean Chamber · Descending Passage

the king reached and flourished in the afterlife. Among these essential aspects were the choice of pyramidal shape and the proper alignment of the monuments. Much effort was also directed toward constructing proper interior chambers for the pharaoh's remains and placing within them the elaborate grave goods that would be buried with him for his use in the next life. At the same time, care was taken to see that the royal body and its accompanying effects would be safe from grave robbers (efforts that unfortunately proved futile most of the time).

The Creation Mound and Sun's Rays

The first religious consideration in the creation of these great tombs was the pyramidal shape itself. When Djoser's royal architect, Imhotep, designed the first pyramid tomb (the Step Pyramid) at the dawn of the Old Kingdom, he did not choose its shape randomly. Rather, that shape possessed at least three divine or mystical meanings, either real or symbolic, in religious tradition and lore. All three were connected to the Sun and its rays, which had special significance in ancient Egyptian religion.

First, the pyramidal shape was linked to the primeval (original, very ancient) mound of creation. This mound was thought to have appeared at Heliopolis, a town and religious site located a few miles northeast of Giza and modern Cairo. The priests of Heliopolis maintained a creation story that explained how the mound came into being. At first the universe consisted only of chaos,

A carved relief shows a pharaoh (left) holding hands with the creator god Atum.

a void often described as a bottomless pit of black water. In some unknown manner, the glorious god Atum sprang into being. He proceeded to create the primeval mound, the first land on Earth. Atum also took the form of the Sun and its rays, which later became associated with the god Ra. In this manifestation, a combination of creator-god and Sun-god, Atum in a sense had morphed into a dual god, Atum-Ra. (Later, the Egyptians substituted Amun for Atum, rendering the dual god Amun-Ra.)

Whether one chose to call the creator-god Atum or Amun, one crucial point was that the primeval mound, or *benben*, he

The three great pyramids at Giza glow in the morning sun. These structures were envisioned in part as ramps to heaven.

had fashioned was supposedly shaped something like a pyramid. A temple at Heliopolis housed a sacred stone that was carefully maintained by the local priests. Appropriately called the *benben* stone, it symbolized the original mound and was pyramidal in shape.

Another crucial religious belief was that the primeval mound was the first thing touched by the golden rays of the creator-god in his manifestation as Ra, the Sun. This made the mound, and with it the pyramidal shape, sacred. And it explains not only why this shape was chosen for so many royal tombs but also why the pyramids were topped by a pyramidion. This capstone was essentially a miniature pyra-mid gilded with metal to reflect the Sun's rays.

The other two major symbolic meanings of the pyramidal shape were related to the first. On the one hand, this shape resembled the triangular flaring effect created when the Sun's rays pierce and fan out from a bank of clouds, a phenomenon commonly seen in Egypt. The late I.E.S. Edwards, one of the world's leading experts on the pyramids, wrote:

A remarkable spectacle may sometimes be seen in the late afternoon of a cloudy winter day at Giza. When standing on the road to Sakkara and gazing west-ward toward the Pyramid plateau, it is possible to see the Sun's rays striking downward through a gap in the clouds at about the same angle as the slope of the Great Pyramid. The impression made on the mind by the scene is that the immaterial prototype [the rays] and the material replica [the pyramid] are here ranged side by side.[15]

A pyramid was also seen in the symbolic sense as a special ramp or stairway. On that ramp, which would eventually merge with rays of sunlight, the pharaoh's spirit would ascend into the heavens. This belief was described by passages from the so-called Pyramid Texts. (The oldest known Egyptian funerary writings, they were carved on the inside of tombs erected in the late Old Kingdom.) One of these texts reads in part:

> A ramp to the sky is built for him [the pharaoh], that he may go up to the sky. . . . He flies as a bird, and he settles as a beetle on the empty seat on the ship of Ra. . . . He has gone up into the sky and has found Ra. . . . He has taken his stand with Ra in the northern part of the sky.[16]

Alignment Toward True North

The phrase "Ra in the northern part of the sky" is significant in that it provides a clue about the physical alignment of the Giza pyramids. All three are nearly perfectly aligned so that the four sides of each structure point directly toward the four cardinal points—north, east, south, and west. The exact reasons for this plan remain unclear. But many scholars think it is revealing that the official entrances to these pyramids are located in the middle of the north faces. It may be that the Egyptians came to believe that the pharaoh's soul must join the gods somewhere in the northern region of the sky. Aligning the pyramids so that they faced due north might ensure that his soul would have a

The orderly alignment of the Giza pyramids is visible in this elevated view.

direct, unobstructed path to its divine destination. (The belief may have been that his spirit passed through a narrow shaft that led from the inner tomb chamber to the pyramid's north face.)

Even if this theory is incorrect, the fact remains that the three Giza pyramids are aligned with the cardinal points. It is natural to ask how the builders managed to achieve this alignment with such tremendous accuracy. Indeed, the north face of Khufu's pyramid deviates from true north by only one-twentieth of a degree; this is equivalent to a clock being off by a mere three seconds each hour.

One possibility is that workmen erected a temporary circular wall in the middle of the worksite and a surveyor stood in the middle of the circle. The wall was tall enough to block his view of everything but the upper part of the star-studded dome of the night sky. The surveyor faced toward the constellations now known as the Big Bear (Ursa Major) and Little Bear (Ursa Minor), as he knew that these always lie in the northern regions of the sky. He also knew that all the stars in that part of the sky appear to circle around a spot occupying true north. Selecting one of these stars, he watched it circle downward until it disappeared behind the wall and marked the spot on the wall. Then he waited while the star continued to move behind the wall, out of his view. When the star, now in the upward swing in its circular path, reappeared above the edge of the wall, the surveyor marked that spot, too. Finally, he stretched a measuring cord between the two marks, reasoning that the

point lying halfway between them would line up with the center of the circle the star made in the sky. That center coincided with true north.

Another method that may have been used either in conjunction with or instead of the one above involved the use of a pole called a gnomon, as explained by Kevin Jackson and Jonathan Stamp:

The pole is stuck in the ground, as close to perfectly vertical as can be achieved with a plumb-line, and its shadow on the ground measured three hours before noon. The length is marked on the ground and used as the radius of a circle. As the Sun rides higher in the sky, the shadow grows shorter, and then, in the afternoon, lengthens again. At the point where the shadow once again touches the circle, it forms an angle with the direction of the first shadow. Once again, the bisection [cutting in half] of the angle gives true north.[17]

A more recent theory was advanced by Kate Spence. In an article published in 2000, she suggests that the surveyors working on Khufu's pyramid found true north by sighting two stars, one in the Big Bear, the other in the Little Bear. They reasoned that an imaginary line connecting these stars passed through the spot marking true north in the sky and aligned the pyramid toward this line. It is possible that all three of these methods were used at one time or another, or even all at once, each to double check the accuracy of the others.

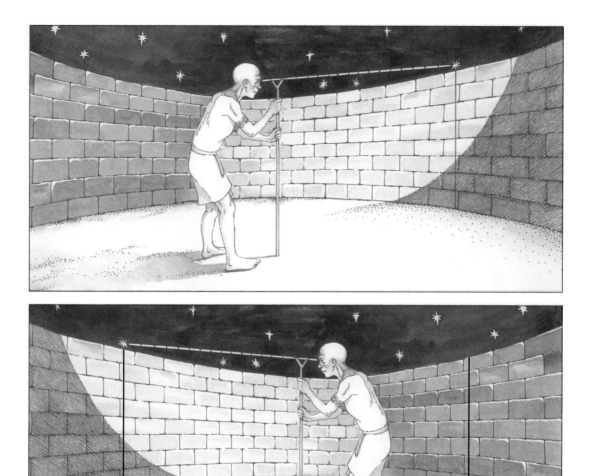

To determine true north, an ancient Egyptian observes a star as it rises in the east (E) and sets in the west (W). The spot halfway between represents true north (N).

Mirroring the Stars?

Another kind of astronomical or mystical alignment relating to the Giza pyramids has frequently been discussed in recent years. Namely, some people have searched for a purposeful pattern in the physical (or spatial) relationship among the three structures. Did their builders have a master plan in which the pyramids' arrangement on the plateau mirrored some celestial, and therefore divine, alignment? If so, it is not based on the cardinal points or even on

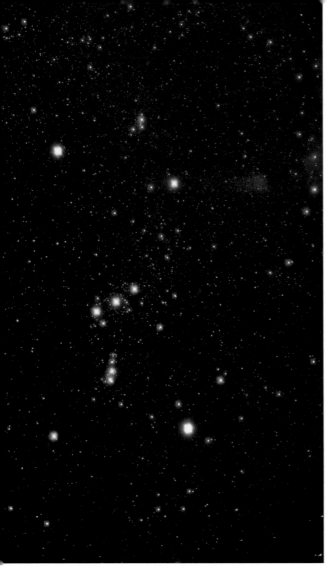

Some people identify the pattern of the stars in Orion's belt with the arrangement of the pyramids.

group. The three bright stars making up the belt of Orion ("the hunter") form a bent line or slight arc similar to that seen in the arrangement of the Giza monuments. However, a number of scholars, including Spence, remain unconvinced. "It is extremely unlikely that there is any master plan," she writes.

> The pyramids were built at different times and as separate projects. Furthermore, the pyramid enclosures are not linked together as one would expect, had the overall plan been important. The diagonal layout is a direct result of the construction process. The pyramids are aligned to true north, and each was therefore built obliquely [at an angle] to the edge of the plateau and set back from the preceding monument both to keep to [remain on] the ridge [plateau] and also to provide a clear view of the northern stars for accurate alignment. [18]

Abandoned Burial Chambers

Whether or not the arrangement of the pyramids on the plateau had any mystical significance, it is certain that the passageways and chambers within these structures had plenty of religious import. After all, the pyramids were intended first and foremost as tombs for Egypt's kings, who for many centuries were seen as divine beings. The interior burial chambers not only housed the royal mummies but also served as launching places from which the pharaohs' souls were thought to ascend

straight lines. An imaginary line drawn through the centers of Khufu's and Khafre's pyramids does not pass through the center of Menkaure's tomb. The latter lies a couple of hundred feet from that line.

The most popular theory attempting to explain this displacement holds that the builders were mimicking a prominent star

Inside the Other Giza Pyramids

Much has been written about the interior passages and chambers of Khufu's pyramid. In this excerpt from an article (in David P. Silverman's Ancient Egypt*), archaeologist Zahi Hawass describes the interiors of Khafre's and Menkaure's pyramids.*

Khafre's pyramid . . . has two entrances, each opening onto a descending passage that leads to a chamber. The lower, earlier passage begins two hundred feet north of the pyramid and was hewn entirely from the solid rock of the plateau. It is linked to the upper passage by an ascending corridor. The lower entrance was abandoned in favor of the upper one. . . . At the end of the upper passageway . . . is the chamber containing Khafre's red granite sarcophagus. Two other tunnels in the pyramid are the work of ancient tomb robbers. . . . From the entrance [of Menkaure's pyramid], on the north side, a descending passage leads to the burial chamber, in which [was] found a basalt sarcophagus that would have originally contained Menkaure's mummy.

The interior of Menkaure's burial chamber features a hole (bottom right) where tomb robbers broke in.

into the heavens. The interiors of these buildings were therefore sacred areas. The authors of a popular book on the pyramids call Khufu's monument, "a machine for the dead, or perhaps more exactly, as a machine for resurrection. The interior structure is an ingenious machine indeed, made up of chambers, antechambers, open passages, hidden passages, shafts, and portcullises [sliding doors]." [19]

In fact, Khufu's pyramid has more internal passages and chambers than any other pyramid constructed during the Old Kingdom. In contrast, the interior plan for Khafre's monument is fairly simple and straightforward. There, a few corridors snake through the lower part of the pyramid to a single burial chamber located beneath the building. An examination of the inside of Khufu's pyramid shows that he and his architect had originally planned for a similar simple arrangement. The entrance in the north face opened into what is now called the Descending Corridor. This 221-foot-long tunnel led to the original crypt, located 98 feet below the plateau's surface. (This chamber measures 46 feet long by 27 feet wide and 11.5 feet high.)

At some point early in the building process, however, Khufu seems to have changed his mind. For reasons that can only be guessed at now, he (or his architect) decided it would be better to place the burial chamber higher, within the actual body of the pyramid. (Perhaps they thought a spot inside the great mass of stone would be harder for tomb robbers to reach.) Thus, the unfinished subterranean chamber was abandoned and a new

passage, the so-called Ascending Corridor, was constructed. The Ascending Corridor runs off the Descending Corridor beginning at a point about 75 feet from the north-face entrance and runs for 129 feet into the heart of the monument. (The Ascending Corridor slants upward part of the way, then levels off.)

At the end of the Ascending Corridor is the second chamber, originally intended to hold Khufu's sarcophagus (stone coffin) and grave goods. In later ages it mistakenly came to be called the Queen's Chamber, and the name stuck, despite the fact that it was built for the pharaoh, not his wife. This room measures 19 feet long by 17 feet wide by a bit more than 20 feet high. It would have made an impressive final resting place for the pharaoh.

Construction of the King's Chamber

However, shortly before the Queen's Chamber was finished, Khufu changed his mind yet again and decided that he wanted his burial chamber to be even higher up in the pyramid. To accommodate this desire, the builders added another upward-slanting corridor beginning at the point where the Ascending Corridor levels off. This new passageway, the largest in the pyramid, is today called the Grand Gallery. This quite amazing piece of architecture is 153 feet long and 28 feet high.

The Grand Gallery is impressive not only for its size but also because it features the finest and most sophisticated corbelled roof created in Egypt during the Old Kingdom.

A nineteenth-century painting depicts men exploring Khufu's burial chamber and its massive stone sarcophagus.

In the corbelling technique, courses of stone are laid so that each course slightly overhangs the one below it. Eventually, they meet at the top. In this case, the final courses narrow to a gap of about three and a half feet, which is topped and filled by a course of flat slabs of polished limestone.

The Grand Gallery leads to the burial chamber that Khufu actually ended up using. Today called the King's Chamber, it is 34 feet long, 17 feet wide, and 19 feet high. In this room, the sarcophagus bearing the pharaoh's mummy was placed following his death, along with huge amounts of food, clothes, weapons, boats, and other goods intended for his use in the afterlife.

Modern tourists who have made their way through the Grand Gallery and into the King's Chamber are often amazed that such large spaces could be carved out of solid stone. This is a misconception, however. With a few minor exceptions, these and the other interior passages and chambers in the pyramid were constructed as the pyramid rose, not tunneled out afterward. For example, an entire room—the Queen's Chamber, for instance—could be erected like a free-standing structure on top of a completed flat course of stones; then new courses of stone could be added around and on top of the finished chamber, in a sense burying it from view. Edwards elaborates:

Today, Khufu's stone sarcophagus shows the wear and tear of decades of tourism.

together on the ground and numbered so that, when they were taken to their final position, they could be reassembled with the minimum of delay.[20]

Part of the proof that this method was employed consists of the dimensions of Khufu's heavy granite sarcophagus. The coffin is wider than the entrance to the Ascending Corridor. This means that it could not have been brought into the pyramid through the network of passages after the structure was complete. It had to have been installed directly into the King's Chamber when that room was still open to the air at an earlier stage of construction. As scholars Peter Clayton and Martin Price quip, Khufu's sarcophagus "qualifies as being the first example of 'built in' furniture in the world."[21]

Trying to Keep Looters Out

Another crucial aspect of the planning and early building stages of the interior of Khufu's pyramid (as well as the insides of other pyramids) was the issue of security. Well before the advent of the Old Kingdom, tomb robbers had regularly pillaged the burial sites of kings and other wealthy people. So the architects and builders who worked at Giza during the Fourth Dynasty were aware of the problem. And they tried to incorporate solutions into their own pyramids.

Contrary to popular opinion, one solution the pharaohs and their builders apparently did not attempt was to place curses on the pyramids or the burial chambers. No

Subsidiary ramps [probably made of wooden timbers], capable of being dismantled in a few hours, could have been erected at any stage convenient, so that blocks could be taken to a considerably greater height than the level of the [larger upper] course under construction. In this way, the men employed would have had time to complete their work on the interior of the pyramid before the surrounding courses of core-masonry had risen to such a height that it would become necessary to roof the corridor and chambers. . . . As a further aid, the stones would be carefully prepared before they were required by the builders. The roofing slabs of the King's Chamber . . . for instance, were fitted

curses have ever been found on or in the three great Giza monuments. In fact, archaeologists say that it was extremely rare for kings to resort to curses to scare away thieves. However, such curses were fairly common in the tombs of lesser government officials and ordinary Egyptians. Zahi Hawass found some in the workers' cemetery near Khufu's pyramid on the Giza plateau, including one guarding the tomb of a man named Petety. "Listen all of you!" the curse warns potential despoilers of the tomb:

> The priest of Hathor [goddess of love] will beat twice any one of you who enters this tomb or does harm to it. The gods will confront him because I am honored by his Lord. The gods will not allow anything to happen to me. Anyone who does anything bad to my tomb, then (the) crocodile, (the) hippopotamus, and the lion will eat him. [22]

It is unclear why the builders of the Giza pyramids did not see fit to use such curses as insurance against thieves. Perhaps they did, but delivered the curses verbally during the funeral ceremony. More plausibly, those who built Khufu's monument probably thought that the physical safeguards they were installing would be more than sufficient to keep looters out.

These precautions included five basic lines of defense, four contained within the structure itself and the fifth outside of it. The first and innermost of these security measures consisted of three doors—actually thick slabs of granite, one positioned directly behind another. At the conclusion

of the funeral ceremony, workers slid these slabs into place directly in front of the King's Chamber, sealing it.

The second line of defense was likely seen as the most formidable. The Grand Gallery was equipped with several more chunks, or plugs, of granite, held back during the construction stages by large wooden beams. As Clayton and Price explain, after the sealing of the King's Chamber,

> the priests [who had conducted the funeral ceremony] retreated and left behind a gang of workmen who proceeded to knock the [beams] away and let the granite plugs fall and slide down [the Grand Gallery] to block the Ascending Corridor. In so doing, of course, they were themselves trapped behind the plugs in the interior of the pyramid. . . . They had, however, an escape route, since it was not the practice to inter [bury] the work force in the Old Kingdom. Their escape route was via a narrow shaft that led from beneath a stone in the upper corridor at the top of the Grand Gallery, down through the body of the pyramid to emerge below the lower corridor. [23]

(Thus, the scene in the popular film *Land of the Pharaohs*, in which the high priests purposely seal themselves, along with Khufu's queen, inside the pyramid, is entertaining but purely fictional.)

The workmen installed the third line of defense by plugging the entrance corridor from the junction of the Ascending and Descending passages to the north-face entrance. The fourth line of defense consisted of a polished casing stone that covered that entrance. This stone blended with the other casing blocks on the north face. And the planners hoped that the exact location of the entrance would be forgotten over time, making it impossible for tomb robbers to find a way in. The last safeguard consisted of placing guards to patrol outside the monument twenty-four hours a day, seven days a week.

The Ravages of Time and Chance

Unfortunately for Khufu, all of these elaborate and labor-intensive precautions proved futile. His tomb, like those of Djoser, Khafre, Menkaure, and most other pharaohs, was desecrated and looted of all its contents.

How could this have happened? First, in spite of the installation of a casing stone over the entrance, the location of the portal was not forgotten. Thousands of workmen and guards knew where it was, and over time this information passed from generation to generation.

Speaking of the guards, Khufu's, Khafre's, and Menkaure's immediate successors probably kept them in place. And the Giza complex likely remained well guarded as long as the kingdom remained stable. But shortly after 2200 B.C. (about three centuries after Menkaure's reign), the Old Kingdom ended with the onset of an era of political instability and disunity. During this roughly 180-year span, which scholars call the First Intermediate Period, numerous power struggles ensued and the seat of government shifted frequently.

A Medieval Breach of Khufu's Tomb

Ancient tomb robbers were not the only ones who tried to enter and loot the great pyramids at Giza. In about the year 810, an Arab caliph named Abdullah Al-Mamun visited Giza with a small army of engineers and stonemasons, hoping to find a way inside Khufu's monument and acquire any treasures stored within. At first, the workers tried hammers and chisels. When this proved too difficult and time consuming, they started huge bonfires beside the pyramid and heated the outer stones until they were red hot. Then they threw cold vinegar onto the hot stones, causing them to crack. A battering ram was then applied. Using this crude but effective method, they managed to tunnel about a hundred feet into the structure. Some accounts claim that Al-Mamun's men continued exploring and eventually found the Queen's and King's Chambers, which were empty, though these stories remain unconfirmed. What is certain is that the initial tunnel they cut survives and is now the main entrance used by tourists visiting the monument.

In a scene from Land of the Pharaohs, *workmen install a granite plug that will block the pyramid's main corridor.*

During this strife, the participants in the ongoing struggles for political survival and dominance likely did not view guarding tombs several centuries old as a priority. And most experts believe that sometime during these unsettled years the Giza monuments were looted. With no one to stop them, gangs of men tunneled through the soft limestone and one by one removed most of the granite plugs that the builders had hoped would seal the tomb forever. Adding insult to injury, it was not long before further pillage of the Giza complex became officially sanctioned. During the Twelfth Dynasty (1985–1795 B.C.), in the Middle Kingdom, builders began removing some of the limestone blocks from the Giza structures for use in the construction of new pyramids (at Lisht, about thirty miles south of Giza).

Vandalism and decay continued. And by the time Herodotus visited Egypt some fourteen centuries later (in the 400s B.C.), the Giza monuments were quaint but decaying and unmaintained tourist attractions. No one, including the natives, remembered exactly when, how, or even why they were built, and only the names of the builders had survived. As has happened so often in history, the ravages of time had steadily undone the most careful planning and strenuous efforts of the mightiest of humans. Nowhere has this inevitable process been summed up better than in the following biblical passage: "I returned and saw under the Sun that the race is not to the swift, nor the battle to the strong . . . but time and chance happen to them all." [24]

Chapter Three

THE COLOSSI: THE SPHINX AND OTHER GIANT STATUES

The pyramids are without doubt the most famous of the monumental structures of ancient Egypt. But the Sphinx at Giza and other colossal stone statues (generally referred to as "colossi") are a close second. The remains of such giant statues have been found all over Egypt. They represented both gods and human leaders, and they adorned temples, palaces, and burial sites alike. The colossi are impressive both for the huge energies that went into sculpting them and for the major difficulties in transporting them. Each weighed dozens, sometimes even hundreds, of tons. And with a few exceptions (notably the Sphinx at Giza, which was carved on the spot), they had to be moved from quarries to their final resting places.

Functions and Meanings of Statues

Statues large and small were carved all across the ancient world, and many examples have survived. Nearly all of these are either beautiful or impressive or both, but they did not all have the same functions and meanings. The differences between the statues of the Greeks and those of the Egyptians are very instructive in understanding why the Egyptians carved these monuments. A few Greek statues were cult figures of gods that stood inside temples and became the focus of worship. But most, whether of gods or humans, were intended as works of art to be admired for their beauty.

In contrast, the vast majority of ancient Egyptian statues, particularly the colossi, had specific religious functions and meanings. Most statues were seen as receptacles, or host vehicles, for a nonphysical being or entity. This entity might be a god or goddess (who was otherwise invisible), part of the soul of a deceased pharaoh, or the spirit of some other dead person. In this view, the statue was a place in the physical world where a spirit could exist and rest and from which it might communicate with living humans. For this reason, it was considered important for sculptors to do their best to capture the physical attributes of the god or person the statue represented. Thus, the numerous colossi erected by the great builder Ramesses II (reigned 1279–1213 B.C.) all across Egypt were not simply giant images endowed with generic features; they actually looked like Ramesses. Similarly, the facial features of a sphinx statue commissioned by Queen Hatshepsut (1473–1458 B.C.), now in New York's Metropolitan Museum of Art, closely resembled her own.

Because of this supposed spiritual habitation of statues, they were most often the focal points of religious rituals. "Offerings were made to them," Egyptologist Gay Robins explains,

> or rather to the being inhabiting them, incense was burned before them, and the correct words were recited and actions performed. In order for the statue to function this way, it had to undergo [a ritual known as] the opening of the mouth . . . which vitalized it and enabled it to house the being it represented. The burning of the incense was important because the

word for "incense," *senetjer,* also meant "to make divine." [25]

The Egyptians carved these religious images from various materials, including wood, metal, and stone. Most of the surviving ones, including the colossi, are of stone, ranging from relatively soft varieties, like limestone and sandstone, to harder

This is one of several colossi of King Ramesses II erected at Luxor.

ones like granite and basalt. In most cases, the sculptors began by selecting a rectangular block of stone. It had to be slightly larger than the projected size of the statue because a certain amount of stone would be removed during the carving process. The sculptors painted outlines of the figure they intended to make directly onto the front, back, and sides of the block. These outlines provided them with a guide to indicate where to cut into the stone using chisels and other metal or stone tools. Robins describes the steps that followed:

[The] sculptors then cut away the stone on all four sides and the top around the sketched outline until they achieved the rough shape of the statue. As they cut the sketch . . . away with the [discarded] stone, they would re-mark important levels and points with lines or dots of paint. Once they had the outline of the statue shaped, they could concentrate on modeling the face and body and executing the details of costume. . . . The eyes were often inlaid with white and

A scene from a 1990s documentary film shows a reenactment of ancient Egyptian sculptors carving statues.

This twenty-five-foot-long sphinx, with the body of a lion and head of a pharaoh, dates from the Eighteenth Dynasty.

black stones . . . and might be surrounded by a copper rim.[26]

Religious and Symbolic Meanings of Sphinxes

Of these finely made products of the Egyptian sculptors, those having the image of a sphinx are probably the most famous and recognizable. The word *sphinx* may have derived from the Egyptian term *she-sep-ankh*, meaning "living image." However, a sphinx was not the image of anything that ever actually lived. It was instead a mythical creature having the combined features of a human and an animal, most often a lion (but also occasionally a ram, hawk, or some other beast). The most common kind of sphinx (including the big one at Giza) was a morph of a specific pharaoh and a lion.

The lion imagery integral to many sphinx statues was not a matter of chance. Dating back well before the Old Kingdom, the lion was closely associated with the living ruler (as was the hawk). The likely reason for this was that lions were known for their strength and ferocity, which made them effective both as predators and guardians; and similarly, people saw it as the king's duty both to guard the nation and to attack its enemies. Moreover, both the lion and the pharaoh were believed to be endowed with divine qualities. Desmond

An avenue lined by ram-headed sphinxes leads to the central gate of a temple. Sphinxes were often associated with sun deities.

Stewart, a specialist in Near Eastern cultures, elaborates:

> A tame lion accompanied the king into battle. Much more than a mascot, he represented the reassuring presence of a god. For the lion had earlier been incorporated into divinity. Ptah, the god of Memphis, belonged to a triad [group of three] whose other members, Nefer-Atum and Sekhmet, both had leonine [lionlike] associations. Nefer-Atum was portrayed standing on a lion, while his mother, Sekhmet, had a lioness's head.[27]

Eventually, the Egyptians also came to associate the image and figure of the sphinx with Sun gods (and solar cults). Some scholars, including German Egyptologist Herbert Ricke, think that this symbolic meaning had evolved by the time of the Fourth Dynasty, whose leading members raised the pyramids at Giza. In this context, a sphinx was seen as a particular manifestation of the Sun god—namely Hor-em-Akhet, or "Horus of the Horizon."

In fact, the Egyptians of the New Kingdom came to call the Great Sphinx at Giza by this name. Here, the "horizon" was the line connecting the bases of Khufu's and Khafre's great pyramids. As one approaches these monuments from the east, the Sphinx's head appears to rest between them, as if framed by them. (Some scholars go a step further and assert that this corresponds with the Egyptian hieroglyph for *horizon*, which represents the Sun rising between two mountains. In this case, when viewed from the proper angle, the Sphinx, a manifestation of the Sun, rests between two human-made mountains, the pyramids.)

The Great Sphinx

These ancient views of sphinxes as semidivine guardians lining the horizons of the Sun frequently motivated Egyptian builders to include large, very heavy sphinx statues in religious architectural settings. For example, rows of big, ram-headed sphinxes lined the processional path leading from the great temple complex at Karnak to the Luxor temple, situated farther south. There must have been many hundreds of them originally because the path was about 1.8 miles long. Similar rows of large sphinxes fronted other temple complexes and individual temples. (For both the 1923 and 1956 versions of *The Ten Commandments*, director Cecil B. DeMille had his art director reproduce such an avenue of giant sphinxes. They were arrayed in front of an accurately reconstructed pair of pylons patterned after those still well preserved in the Temple of Horus at Edifu, about sixty miles south of Thebes.)

The largest sphinx of all, of course, was the one at Giza. The consensus of scholarly opinion is that it was carved during Khafre's reign as part of his funerary complex, which included, in addition to his

Thutmose's Dream

One of the most famous ancient tales about the Great Sphinx at Giza involves the pharaoh Thutmose IV, who reigned from about 1400 to 1390 B.C. A red granite stele found near the chest of the Sphinx tells how, when he was still a young prince, Thutmose fell asleep beside the monument. In a dream, the Sphinx came to him and said:

Look at me, Thutmose, my son. I am your father, Horus of the Horizon. I promise what is in my [power to give]: Earthly rule at the head of all the living. Seated on the throne . . . you will wear the White Crown and the Red. All the territory on which the eye of the Sun rests will be yours. *(Quoted from Stewart's* The Pyramids and Sphinx.*)*

All this and more would be Thutmose's, the Sphinx promised, despite the fact that the young man was only second in line to inherit the throne. But first, he must pledge to clear the sand that had begun to envelop the monument and make other repairs. Thutmose did become king, and he completed the restoration of the Sphinx. Many historians think that the pharaoh concocted this tale to justify his kingship following the premature death of his elder brother, who had been first in line to the throne.

pyramid, a number of temples, causeways, and statues. In recent years some popular writers have suggested that the Great Sphinx was built long before Khafre's time by a civilization that predated that of the Egyptians in the area. However, no reliable evidence has yet been found to support the existence of such a civilization.

Furthermore, the physical characteristics and spatial context of the Sphinx solidly link it to Khafre. The statue's pose, facial features, and accessories match those of a

Oedipus and the Sphinx

Centuries after its completion, the Great Sphinx at Giza, along with the image of Egyptian sphinxes in general, inspired stories of sphinxes in other eastern Mediterranean lands. Probably the best known are those of the Greeks, who visualized the sphinx as a frightening monster having the body of a winged lion and the face of a human woman. In one famous tale, the Greek city of Thebes was plagued by a bloodthirsty sphinx that would leap out at travelers and pose them a riddle. If a person could solve the riddle, the monster promised it would let him or her go. But if not, the person would be devoured. No one could solve the riddle, and many people met grisly deaths in the creature's clutches. Eventually, a young man named Oedipus, a native of the city of Corinth, appeared. He bravely confronted the monster, which demanded that he solve the riddle. According to the first-century B.C. Greek historian Diodorus Siculus (in volume four of his *Library of History*), this was the riddle: "What is it that is of itself two-footed, three-footed, and four-footed?" The shrewd Oedipus immediately answered "man" because "as an infant man begins to move as a four-footed being [crawling on all fours], when he is grown he is two-footed, and as an old man he is three-footed, leaning upon a staff because of his weakness." Devastated at being outwitted by a human, the sphinx cried out in despair and committed suicide. Afterward, the grateful Thebans made Oedipus king of their city.

In a nineteenth-century painting, Oedipus confronts the Sphinx.

smaller statue of Khafre found in one of his temples at Giza. The head was (and still is) wrapped in a pleated headdress (the *nemes*). It originally sported a cobra above the brow, a symbol associated with royalty; but this, and another symbolic accessory, a false beard (linked to the god Osiris) were hacked off (or fell off) in ancient times. The nose is also missing, lopped off by a medieval Arab cleric who viewed the Sphinx as an ungodly idol.

The Sphinx is about 66 feet high from the top of its head to the foot of its base, and it is roughly 240 feet, not far short of a football field, in length. It is composed primarily of low-quality limestone, part of a rocky outcrop that already stood on the spot before the Giza plateau became a building site. The outcrop lay in the center of a quarry. So the workers accomplished two tasks at once, saving much time and effort; as they cut away stone blocks for use in various Giza structures, they simultaneously cleared the space around the great statue, delineating its general form and shape. Some of the stones excavated from the areas near the Sphinx were used to construct a temple (appropriately called the Sphinx Temple) situated only a few dozen feet in front of the statue.

The Sphinx was the first of the colossal statues created in Egypt. That meant that the builders had no prior experience to guide them through the difficulties of such an enormous and specialized project. This factor, combined with the general shape and low quality of the onsite limestone outcrop, make the monument artistically inferior to many later colossi (though still impressive for its sheer size). "The Sphinx is, in fact, not particularly well proportioned," Kate Spence points out.

The body is too long and head too small. The ancient sculptors may have been constrained [limited] by their material. The size of the head will have been limited by the size of the natural rock nodule from which it was carved, and the body may have been lengthened following the discovery of a vertical fault, now running just in front of the back legs. However, the strange proportions also testify to the inexperience of the sculptor. . . . Odd proportions in some life-size statuary of the period shows that the Egyptians had not yet developed the . . . systems [for creating the proper proportions] used so successfully in later sculpture. [28]

Other Well-Known Colossi

Clearly, the Sphinx is so huge and heavy that it could never have been moved in one piece, even if that had been part of the original plan. Many other ancient Egyptian colossi were moved, however, a seemingly amazing feat considering their often enormous bulk. Consider the following examples, whose remains became popular tourist attractions in Greek and Roman times. (They still are today, although some were removed from Egypt over the centuries and now rest in museums around the world.)

At the same time that some of Khafre's sculptors were carving the Great Sphinx out of the Giza plateau, others were working on giant statues of the pharaoh. The doors to his funerary temple at Giza were flanked by four huge sphinxes, each about twenty-six feet long. In addition, the temple itself originally housed many colossal statues of Khafre, in either sitting or standing poses, at least seven of them inside and another twelve outside. Similar colossi adorned the pyramid complex of Khafre's successor, Menkaure. A huge sitting statue of Menkaure, fashioned from white alabaster, has survived in excellent condition and now rests in the Museum of Fine Arts in Boston.

Two statues that closely resemble Menkaure's alabaster one, except that they are

One of the large sphinxes of Amenemhat III.

even larger, are still in Egypt. They were commissioned by a Middle Kingdom pharaoh, Amenemhat III (1855–1808 B.C.). (He is famous for building a pyramid that collapsed the year it was finished, forcing him to build another.) Erected to celebrate his completion of a canal, the two colossi weigh between eleven and thirteen tons each and had to be transported from a distant quarry. Amenemhat also had a number of large black granite sphinxes made of himself, some of which have survived. Each sphinx rests on a solid rectangular base, for a combined weight of several tons.

These and other similar large-scale statues are impressive, to be sure. Yet they were relatively small compared to a number of other colossi, some of which have survived in various states of preservation (or are represented in surviving art). During the Middle Kingdom, for instance, a wealthy government official named Djehuithotep ordered the creation of a huge statue of himself. It weighed a whopping fifty-eight tons and had to be transported more than twelve miles across the desert before it could be loaded onto a ship for further transport.

The Giants of Thebes and Abu Simbel

Even Djehuithotep's bulky monument pales in comparison to that of some truly enormous Egyptian colossi. The New Kingdom pharaoh Amenhotep III (1390–1352 B.C.) created two that are more than fifty feet high and weigh more than seven hundred tons each. They had to be moved more than four hundred miles from their quarry to their final resting places—the southern and northern flanks of the entrance to Amenhotep's temple in western Thebes. But only the temple's foundations have survived. So the two statues, which depict the pharaoh sitting on his throne with his hands resting palms down on his knees, now loom by themselves, lonely but dominating presences in the otherwise flat fields that surround them.

A fascinating story surrounded these monuments in Greek and Roman times. Modern archaeologists believe that an earthquake damaged one of them in 27 B.C. and caused some odd crack or flaw to form in the stone. Thereafter, various Greek and Roman writers reported that each morning an eerie whistling sound emanated from the statue, which made the site a popular tourist attraction. The sound was probably produced by breezes that passed through the crack and were somehow amplified by daily expansion and contraction of the stone (due to changing temperatures). However, most of the ancients who visited the site were convinced that they were hearing a supernatural voice. The Greeks, who by that time lived in large numbers in Egypt, claimed the mythical Greek character Memnon was singing to his mother, Eos, goddess of the dawn. For this reason, Amenhotep's statues became known as the Colossi of Memnon, a name still used by some people today. In the third century, a Roman emperor, Septimius Severus, repaired the two statues; and thereafter, not surprisingly, the mysterious voice ceased permanently.

Though huge, the Colossi of Memnon were not the largest of ancient Egypt's giant

The badly weathered Colossi of Memnon tower over the plain.

statues. Ramesses II, one of that nation's greatest builders, erected several colossi of himself that dwarf all others except for the Great Sphinx at Giza. In western Thebes, not far from Amenhotep's temple, Ramesses built a temple that featured a statue sixty-two feet tall. It weighed an incredible one thousand tons! Several centuries later its upper section collapsed (probably during an earthquake), and it was the sight of this fallen giant that inspired these famous words of the nineteenth-century English poet Percy Bysshe Shelley:

I met a traveler from an antique land
Who said: Two vast and trunkless legs
   of stone
Stand in the desert. Near them on the
   sand,
Half sunk, a shattered visage lies. [29]

The four enormous colossi of Ramesses II at Abu Simbel attract huge crowds each year. One was damaged by an earthquake in ancient times.

Bigger still were four unfinished colossi of Ramesses, which survive only in fragments. If they had been completed, they would have stood perhaps between seventy and eighty feet high and weighed well over one thousand tons.

The largest of all the great statues created by Ramesses were four truly enormous ones that adorn the front facade of his great temple at Abu Simbel (about 170 miles south of Aswan, in southern Egypt). They are seventy-two feet high. And though their weights are uncertain, each (along with its rectangular base) likely surpasses fifteen hundred tons. Like Amenhotep's colossi at Thebes, each shows the pharaoh sitting with his hands on his knees and staring outward toward a distant horizon. Unlike Amenhotep's statues, however, the giants of Abu

Simbel were never moved by the builders. Like the Great Sphinx, they were carved in place from existing rock formations. (The entire Abu Simbel temple, including the four colossi, did move in the late 1960s, when the creation of a dam and artificial lake threatened to submerge it. At a huge cost in money, time, and energy, the monument was cut into pieces and reassembled at a safe location on higher ground.)

Moving the Giant Statues

Although Ramesses' colossi at Abu Simbel did not have to be moved right after they were carved, many others he commissioned, as well as those of Amenemhat, Djehuit-hotep, and Amenhotep, were moved, often great distances. The Egyptians managed such feats mainly through muscle power, aided by crude wooden sledges. This is shown by a surviving painting in Djehuithotep's tomb that shows the transport of his fifty-eight-ton colossus. In the scene, the statue rests on a large wooden sledge to which four ropes are attached. Forty-three men pull each rope, for a total of 172 men.

At first glance, this number of workers may seem surprisingly small considering the large scale of the undertaking. However, the tomb painting also shows a man standing on the front of the sledge and pouring a liquid in front of it as it moves. Modern experiments in which gangs of laborers pulled large stones on sledges confirm that water or other liquids greatly reduce the friction of the sledges as they move along their tracks. These experiments have shown that, with the reduced friction, one worker can fairly easily drag one-third of a ton. This almost exactly matches the weight-to-worker ratio depicted in Djehuithotep's tomb, in which 172 men move a fifty-eight-ton statue. Using the same ratio, Amenhotep's seven hundred-ton colossi would each require about 2,100 men to haul across the desert. This is admittedly a large workforce, but one that any pharaoh would have had no trouble assembling, even on short notice.

Once a giant statue had been transported and installed in its final resting place, artisans added the finishing touches. Carving fine details, polishing, and painting were usually left to this stage since the surfaces of the statues could easily incur minor damage during the long and difficult transport stage. Because most of these colossi were far taller than the tallest person, scaffolding was required for the artisans to stand on. Fortunately, a painted scene showing such scaffolding has survived in the tomb of Rekhmira, a high official under the pharaoh Thutmose III (1479–1425 B.C.). As Dieter Arnold describes it, "The scaffolding consists of light poles, tied together by knots of

Workmen move a colossus toward the entrance of a temple at Karnak in this modern painting.

Some American Sphinxes Lost and Found

In 1923 the legendary Hollywood director Cecil B. DeMille released his first version of *The Ten Commandments*. He wanted to shoot on location in Egypt, but his studio, Paramount, told him it would be too expensive. Instead, he filmed large portions of the set exteriors in some huge sand dunes in Guadalupe, California (about 170 miles north of Los Angeles). The main set, one of the largest ever constructed for a film, reproduced two mammoth pylons and an avenue of stone sphinxes from the reign of Ramesses II. There were forty-two sphinxes, each weighing five tons. When the shooting was over, workmen covered the set with sand to keep other filmmakers from utilizing it. DeMille later joked in his memoirs that he hoped that a thousand years in the future archaeologists would find the sphinxes and conclude that the ancient Egyptians had colonized North America. In the 1980s and 1990s, archaeologists did find DeMille's old set and partially excavated it, although they had no illusions about who had built it!

Part of one of DeMille's mammoth modern film sets.

rope, the primitive but efficient methods also used in medieval cathedral building."[30] A more elaborate version of the same sort of scaffolding was probably used in the carving of the upper sections of the stationary Great Sphinx and Abu Simbel colossi.

After the artisans completed their work, the scaffolding was removed. And people stood in awe of the towering images of their gods and rulers, for in those days it was thought that only the mighty and the divine could inspire such immense works. However, as in the case of the pyramids and their builders, time, the great leveler, did its work. Shelley stated it well in the conclusion of his poem about the fallen giant at Thebes. The builder, Shelley said, had once called himself the "King of Kings" and boasted, "Look on my works, ye mighty, and despair!" Yet now, "round the decay of that colossal wreck, boundless and bare, the lone and level sands stretch far away."[31]

Chapter Four

TIES TO THE DIVINE: TEMPLES, OBELISKS, AND PALACES

Often no less impressive than pyramids and giant statues, ancient Egypt's temples were stone monuments whose majestic ruins awed early modern Western visitors to that land (and continue to awe people today). It has been established that the ancient Egyptians were religiously devout in the extreme. So it is not surprising that a large portion of their national wealth and energies went into erecting great shrines to their gods.

Building a temple or adding to an existing one was also a way for a pharaoh to demonstrate his connection to the divine and thereby to enhance his prestige. In fact, during the New Kingdom it became customary for each new pharaoh to engage in some kind of temple construction. The most spectacular result was the mammoth temple complex at Karnak (near Thebes), primarily dedicated to Amun-Ra, chief god in the New Kingdom era. "It was considered each king's duty," Kate Spence explains,

to build or aggrandize [enlarge] the temples of the gods, and the importance of Amun-Ra ensured that most [New Kingdom] kings left their mark somewhere at Karnak. The small Middle Kingdom shrine [that originally occupied the site] rapidly expanded outwards, as pyloned gateways, columned halls, and subsidiary temples were built around it and adorned with relief decoration, statuary, and obelisks. . . . Today, the ruined temples provide a wealth of information on the techniques used by the ancient Egyptians to build freestanding stone structures.[32]

Spence mentions obelisks adorning the Karnak temples. Indeed, these tall, tapering needles of stone were associated almost exclusively with temples. Pairs of giant obelisks usually flanked the temple doors—these doors were situated in the centers of the temples beneath the characteristic flat-topped gateways called pylons. The pillars inside the temples were often huge. But from a construction standpoint, they were not nearly as impressive as the obelisks standing outside. This is because a pillar was erected by stacking several smaller stone blocks; an obelisk, however, was usually quarried, transported, and raised as a single, incredibly heavy block.

Another large-scale architectural form associated with temples in ancient Egypt was the palace. Palaces most often physically adjoined temples. On the one hand, this allowed a pharaoh to walk to and from the two structures most central to the government in a matter of minutes. More importantly, it further strengthened the king's perceived ties to divine forces.

Mortuary Temples

This traditionally accepted connection between the pharaoh and the gods cannot

A reconstruction for a modern book accurately captures a panorama of buildings in and around the Karnak temple complex.

The Propaganda Value of Temple Building

Pride and propaganda were likely two of the reasons why the New Kingdom pharaoh Amenhotep III ordered that the inscription quoted in part below (translated by J.H. Breasted in volume 2 of his Ancient Records of Egypt*) be placed in the temple he built on the Nile's west bank at Thebes.*

Behold, the heart of his majesty was satisfied with making a very great monument . . . an eternal, everlasting fortress of fine white sandstone, wrought with gold throughout; its floor is adorned with silver, all its portals with electrum [an alloy of gold and silver]; it is made very wide and large, and established forever; and adorned with this very great [stele]. [The temple] contains numerous royal statues, of Elephantine granite, of costly gritstone, of every splendid costly stone, established as everlasting works. Their stature shines more than the heavens, their rays are in the faces of men like the Sun, when he shines early in the morning. . . . It resembles the horizon in heaven when [the god] Ra rises therein. Its lake is filled with the great Nile, lord of fish and fowl.

be overstated in any examination of why and how temples were built in Egypt. A pharaoh who either erected or enlarged a temple did so partly to honor a god or gods. But there was also an element of personal pride, as well as official propaganda, involved. Clearly, any leader who could afford to erect an edifice so large and magnificently decorated was one to be respected, perhaps even feared. Accordingly, King Amenhotep III ordered the addition of a stele bearing a boastful inscription to be placed in a prominent place in the temple he built on the Nile's west bank at Thebes. It reads in part:

Behold, the heart of his majesty was satisfied with making a very great monument; never has happened the like since the beginning [of time]. He made it as his monument for his father, [the creator-god] Amun, lord of Thebes, making for him an august temple on the west of Thebes, an eternal, everlasting fortress of fine white sandstone, wrought with gold throughout; its floor is adorned with silver. . . . It contains numerous royal statues.[33]

This structure that Amenhotep erected at Thebes was a mortuary temple, one of the two main temple types in ancient Egypt. A mortuary temple (which the Egyptians called *hwt*, meaning "mansion") was not intended as a place for general worship of the gods. Rather, it was built as a memorial to and spiritual aid for a king (or queen). The priests who staffed a mortuary temple prayed and made offerings in order to nourish and sustain the monarch's spirit in the afterlife.

Two basic styles of mortuary temple developed in Egypt. The first was prevalent during the Old and Middle Kingdoms and was usually associated with pyramid tombs. The best-preserved example—the mortuary temple of the pharaoh Khafre at Giza—is also fairly typical in its layout for this kind of temple. It features an entrance hall lined with columns; beyond that an open courtyard; at the rear of the courtyard a row of indented niches (where statues of the pharaoh probably stood); behind the niches a storeroom; and in the rear of the temple a small chamber in which priests made offerings for the king's spirit.

The mortuary temples that developed during the New Kingdom were not associated with pyramids (which were no longer built) and followed a different plan. Here again, the best-preserved example is also stylistically fairly typical of the genre. Called Medinet Habu, it is a temple complex erected primarily by Ramesses III (reigned 1184–1153 B.C.) on the Nile's west bank near Thebes. The complex is surrounded by a large rectangular wall (about 650 by 1,000 feet) made of mud bricks. Well inside the walls rests the temple proper, fronted by two massive pylons with the main gate between them. Behind these pylons is an open courtyard. And beyond it is a second (and smaller) set of pylons, which leads to a second courtyard. A door in the back of this courtyard opens into an impressive hypostyle hall. (A central feature of Egyptian religious architecture, a hypostyle hall, from Greek words meaning "resting on pillars," is a covered courtyard in which the roof is held up by rows of columns that fill most of the chamber. This contrasts markedly with most Greek and Roman temples, in which most or all of the pillars holding up the roof stand along the perimeter.) Finally, the rear section of the temple features a large suite of interconnected rooms; these consist of a treasury, a chamber for making offerings for the king, and several chapels.

Cult Temples

The second general temple type in ancient Egypt was the cult temple, in which direct worship of one or more gods took place. (In ancient times, a "cult" consisted of the overall trappings of the worship of a particular god, including shrines, temples, statues of the god, priests, holy objects, and congregations of worshippers.) Unfortunately, the vast majority of the cult temples of the Old and Middle Kingdoms have not survived. And the few that have are in an advanced state of ruin. So it is difficult to tell if there was a common or typical plan or style for these structures. Some scholars suggest that they more or less followed the style of mortuary temples like that of Khafre at Giza. Others think these buildings had no common type, varying widely in layout. It does seem likely that most or all were built using a mix of materials—mud bricks, wooden timbers, and, in some cases, stone.

In contrast, the New Kingdom cult temples were composed almost exclusively of stone. Certainly this is one reason that many of them have survived in reasonably good condition. A more or less standard style emerged for cult temples in this period (and remained common far beyond, down into the Greek and Roman periods). It is well represented in the temple built for the Theban moon god, Khonsu, by Ramesses III at Karnak. Noted archaeologist Steven Snape describes it, while cautioning that the New Kingdom architects often spun off variations of this basic layout:

A massive pylon gateway stands in front of an open colonnaded [column-lined] courtyard, at the back of which a densely columned hypostyle hall acts as a screen in front of the sanctuary [sacred area] which housed the divine image. These four elements (pylon, courtyard, hypostyle hall, and sanctu-ary) are the basic parts of a standard-plan temple. However, the . . . standard plan was probably never thought of by the Egyptians as a firm blueprint for temple design. . . . Variations on the theme were the norm rather than the exception, especially in major temples, like Karnak, which were added to and altered by successive kings. [34]

Thus, cult and mortuary temples had many similar design features during the New Kingdom. These included sets of pylons in front, open courtyards, hypostyle halls, and sacred areas in the rear parts of the structures. The main difference seems to have been the layout of these rear sacred

The mortuary temple of Queen Hatshepsut (reigned ca. 1473–1458 B.C.) is among the best-preserved temples in Egypt.

areas. In cult temples they tended to consist of one or a few chambers devoted to worship of a god or gods. In mortuary temples, in contrast, the sacred areas contained more chambers with more varied functions, almost all related to the welfare of the pharaoh.

Some Nonstandard Temples

Not all Egyptian temples followed these standard layouts and styles. A few were atypical, either because the religious practices involved were unusual or because the physical conditions of the sites chosen for the structures dictated a different style. The most prominent example of a temple based on atypical religious practices was the one erected by the New Kingdom pharaoh Amenhotep IV in the 1340s B.C. A true maverick among Egyptian rulers, he came to believe that there was only one god. This was Aten, whose face was the Sun's blindingly bright disk. Abandoning all the former gods, the pharaoh changed his name to Akhenaten (meaning "Servant of Aten"), departed the traditional capital of Memphis, and built a new capital—Akhetaten ("Horizon of Aten"), today known as Amarna.

The magnificent cult temple Akhenaten built to honor Aten no longer exists. (It was totally dismantled after his death, when later pharaohs rejected his new faith and tried to erase all his works and even the

This huge set built for Cecil B. DeMille's 1956 version of The Ten Commandments *was based on an actual ancient temple.*

Pylons Repel the Forces of Chaos

The pylons that flanked the outer doors of many Egyptian temples, especially during the New Kingdom, had a number of symbolic meanings and functions. In general form, for example, they were truncated (sawed-off) triangles and were therefore related to pyramids, which possessed religious significance. Scholar Richard H. Wilkinson elaborates in this passage from his book about Egyptian temples.

The twin-towered pylon gateways of the developed Egyptian Temple are without doubt the most distinctive architectural feature of these ancient religious structures. . . . The massive structure of the completed pylons clearly served a defensive . . . function, not only physically defending the gateway from intruders, but also symbolically standing as a bastion repelling the . . . forces of chaos and evil in the outer world. . . . The pylon [also] mimicked the shape of the *akhet*, or horizon hieroglyph, or at least was viewed as such, for it was here that the Sun rose on the physical horizon between the outer world and the hidden, sacred landscape of the temple.

---

memory of his rule.) Fortunately, however, in the hills surrounding the Amarna site archaeologists found the tombs of some of Akhenaten's leading courtiers. Paintings on the walls of these tombs show detailed depictions of portions of the now lost city, including the temple complex, called the House of Aten. It appears to have consisted of two distinct structures. The first, called "the Place Where the Aten Is Found," had a standard pylon and open courtyard arrangement in front. But the courtyard contained numerous tablelike altars on which offerings were made to Aten.

The second structure making up the temple complex seems to have been a raised platform bearing a sacred stone. Sacrificial offerings were probably made here as well. Thus, unlike the situation in standard temples, where worship was secretively directed toward statues in enclosed rear chambers, the Amarna temple featured overt outdoor worship directed upward toward the Sun's disk. (But though this worship took place in the open, ordinary Egyptians were not privy to it; they were not allowed past the front gates, and the ceremonies in the courtyard were conducted solely by members of the royal family and selected priests.)

Perhaps the most remarkable of Egypt's nonstandard temples are the two at Abu Simbel, in front of which rest the great colossi of Ramesses II. These cult temples were not created in the usual manner—by assembling vast collections of quarried stones. Instead, they were carved out of a set of imposing cliff faces overlooking the Nile. The great archaeologist Zahi Hawass, who directed studies at Abu Simbel during the 1970s, gives this overall description of the exterior and interior of the larger of the two structures:

> The southern temple . . . [features] an enormous pylon-shaped façade . . . cut back into the pinkish stone of the cliff. Steps lead up to a ledge decorated with sculptures of falcons as symbols of the Sun god. . . . This ledge extends across the façade of the temple in front of four colossal seated figures of Ramesses. . . . The entrance to the temple leads to a corridor whose walls are engraved with images of [the pharaoh]. . . . Doors in the northern wall of the hall open into rooms that appear to have been used as storerooms. . . . In the center of the western wall . . . is a doorway leading to a second, smaller room . . . [with] walls and columns decorated with religious scenes. [35]

The second hall leads to a third, which in turn leads to the inner sanctuary, where the main religious sacrifice took place.

Temple Construction

Excluding temples cut from cliffs like those at Abu Simbel, one thing that Egypt's mortuary and cult temples had in common was the construction methods used to raise them. With a few exceptions, the same basic materials and techniques of pyramid building were employed for temples. Blocks of stone were quarried, dressed, and transported to the worksite. And gangs of workers, guided by architects and overseers, slowly but steadily assembled the temples.

One exception was the size of the stones used. Many (though certainly not all) of the stone blocks used in temples were smaller, and therefore lighter and easier to lift and maneuver, than the ones in large pyramids. The stones used by Akhenaten's builders at Amarna were even smaller than those employed in most temples and resembled large bricks. Here, the smaller stones were chosen because the pharaoh was building a temple, palace, and city from scratch and wanted the structures to rise as quickly as possible; using these smaller stones allowed the work to progress much faster than in standard stone construction,

The well-preserved central corridor of the Abu Simbel temple is lined with colossi.

The pyramids were built on solid bedrock, as seen in this shot from Land of the Pharaohs. *Temples often lacked such strong foundations.*

which used blocks weighing many tons each.

Another common characteristic of temple construction was the use of connecting devices to hold together adjoining blocks and thereby give added stability to the structure. Such connectors are occasionally seen in pyramids. But they are much more numerous in the walls and columns of temples (and palaces, fortresses, and other similar structures). The most common connectors were clamps made of copper or bronze and dovetail shaped (wider at the ends than in the middle). Workmen chiseled or drilled holes in appropriate spots on the tops or sides of adjoining stone blocks and inserted the clamps. (Wooden clamps and stone dowels were also used as connectors, though less often than the metal variety.)

One common construction technique used in many temples and similar stone structures in the New Kingdom ended up reducing rather than increasing their stability. Many of the pyramids and other large stone structures of the Old and Middle Kingdoms were built atop solid bedrock. That gave strong and even support for the enormous weight of the thousands or, in some cases, millions of stones above. In the New Kingdom, however, as Dieter Arnold explains, builders developed "the unfortunate custom of building up the foundation in several courses of rather small blocks." One reason for this practice was "the availability of reusable material from older buildings." These sorts of foundations often lacked the strength and evenness needed to resist the great weight placed on them, Arnold points out.

Ties to the Divine: Temples, Obelisks, and Palaces 65

Quite frequently, column drums, stelae, and even sculptures were packed into such foundations. . . . They certainly do not add to the stability of the construction, because a slightly uneven placement of such stones leads to uneven pressure and cracking of the overlaying blocks.[36]

The Sacred Significance of Obelisks

In contrast, obelisks almost always had wide, very solid stone bases. Such firm foundations were essential because these towering stone needles were extremely heavy. Consider that the relatively small obelisks raised by King Thutmose I (reigned 1504–1492 B.C.) at Karnak weighed 143 tons each. Later, Queen Hatshepsut installed a pair weighing 323 tons each in the same temple complex. Her immediate successor, Thutmose III, created numerous huge obelisks, one (now on display in Istanbul, Turkey) weighs 380 tons; the other (now in Rome) weighs a whopping 455 tons. Largest of all was an unfinished obelisk (commissioned by Thutmose III) that still rests in its quarry southeast of Aswan. If it had been completed, it would have weighed an astonishing 1,168 tons! (The obelisk was abandoned because it had developed a crack that would have made it unstable and prone to collapse when raised.)

Obelisks like these were not meant merely as impressive decoration. Their form had underlying astrological and religious meanings that were directly related to those associated with the pyramids. Like a pyramid, an obelisk had a square base that tapered upward to a pyramidion, the shape symbolizing the sacred *benben* stone (representing the primeval mound) at Heliopolis. Just as the rays of the first rising Sun (at the beginning of time) were believed to have struck the sacred mound, the top section of an obelisk was intended to catch the Sun's rays in early morning. To this end, the pyramidion at the apex was usually gilded with sheets of copper or bronze to reflect the solar rays more effectively. (It was also customary to carve figures of baboons onto an obelisk's base; according to tradition, the Egyptians observed that wild baboons chattered excitedly at sunrise.) It is not surprising, therefore, that obelisks were closely associated with the worship of the various manifestations of the solar god, Ra. And this is why so many obelisks were raised at Karnak, the most spectacular temple complex dedicated to Amun-Ra.

The religious desire to make obelisks look like they were glowing in the Sun's rays often affected the choice of stone used for these monuments. The most popular type was Aswan granite. It has a distinct pinkish tone that produces the desired glowing effect, especially in early morning and late afternoon.

Quarrying, Transporting, and Raising Obelisks

Thutmose III's unfinished obelisk at Aswan not only exemplifies the use of pinkish granite, but it also provides modern scholars valuable clues about how these stone needles were quarried. After a foreman marked the outline of the obelisk on the granite's surface, workers dug a trench on either side. Their primary tool was a ball-shaped pounder made of a type of stone harder than granite (often dolerite). The pounder crushed the granite's surface into small pieces and eventually powder, which other workers removed. Though difficult and tedious, this method was effective. Inch by agonizing inch, the trenches defining the obelisk's sides deepened.

Maneuvering carefully in the narrow trenches, the workers eventually cleared the stone slightly below and beneath the bottom edge of the obelisk. They continued removing granite from the underside of the big needle until it rested on only a few remaining central supports of granite (aided by some temporary wooden timbers). Then the men inserted huge timber levers into the trenches and pried the monument loose. (The protruding remains of the granite supports on the bottom-facing side were later pounded and ground off, leaving a flat surface.)

The next step was to move the obelisk to its destination, a daunting task to say the least. Again using large levers and the muscle power of many workers, the huge stone was maneuvered onto a massive wooden sledge and dragged to the nearby river. Because of their enormous weight, the easiest way to transport obelisks long distances was to float them downstream on large barges.

But how did the workers manage to move an obelisk from its sledge and onto a barge? Fortunately, the first-century A.D. Roman scholar Pliny the Elder had

An unfinished obelisk rests in a quarry at Aswan.

access to information about how one of Egypt's last pharaohs (the second ruler in the Greek Ptolemaic dynasty, who reigned from 285 to 246 B.C.) transported a 120-foot-tall obelisk by ship to Alexandria. First, workers dug a narrow canal that ran from the edge of the quarry to the Nile. Then, they maneuvered the obelisk, which was still lying on its side, so that it laid across the width of the canal, almost like a bridge. In the next step, Pliny writes,

two wide barges were loaded with cubes of granite—each one with a side

The raising of an obelisk, as reenacted in a spectacular scene in DeMille's 1956 film The Ten Commandments.

of one foot—until the weight of the blocks was double that of the obelisk, their total volume being also twice as great. The ships were thus able to float beneath the obelisk, which was suspended by its ends from both banks of the canal. Then the blocks of granite were unloaded and the lightened barges [rose higher in the water until their decks touched the underside and] took the weight of the obelisk. [37]

Pliny reported that workers set up Ptolemy's obelisk on a base made of six granite supports cut from the same quarry. The job of raising such a stone from a horizontal position to a vertical one on its base was the most difficult of all the steps involved. A number of theories have been proposed to explain how the Egyptians accomplished this phenomenal task. To date, the most convincing is that proposed by the early twentieth-century German scholar Ludwig Borchardt. He concluded that workers pulled the obelisk (on a sledge) up close to the edge of the base and carefully inserted the bottom edge of the obelisk into a shallow groove cut into the base's outer edge. Then, using large timber levers, they slowly tilted the monument upward. Eventually, they attached ropes to the upper sections of the obelisk, which large gangs of workers on the other side of the base pulled on until the great needle stood upright on the base.

Ritualistic and Ceremonial Palaces

In addition to pylons, open courtyards, and obelisks, another large-scale structure closely associated with temples in ancient Egypt was the palace. Today, the word *palace* conjures up images of massive, splendidly decorated mansions in which kings and queens resided. But most of the so-called palaces that adjoined the great temples in Egypt

Ramesses III's temple at Medinet Habu, seen in this reconstruction, had an attached palace.

were not used to house the king and his family. (With a few exceptions, the royals actually lived in a separate mansion, appropriately called the *per-aa,* or "great house," the term from which the title *pharaoh* derived during the early New Kingdom.)

Instead, most of the palaces had other functions. Some were ritualistic—that is, they enhanced the religious meaning of the temples to which they were attached. Others were ceremonial, built to house official state ceremonies, including greeting foreign dignitaries. Apparently some, including the palace adjoining the Medinet Habu temple, fulfilled both functions. A central feature of such palaces was "the window of appearance." As Egyptologist Ian Shaw explains, this consisted

> of a ceremonial window at which the king appeared in order to undertake such activities as the reception of visitors, the conducting of ceremonies, or the dispensing of rewards to his loyal courtiers. In the case of the small palaces . . . the window represented a visual threshold between the sacred and profane aspects of the king's rule, a means of passing between palace and temple, the two most important institutions in the central government of Pharaonic Egypt. [38]

Beyond these basic facts, little is known about the structure and uses of these palaces. This is because most were not built of durable stone, as were obelisks and the majority of big temples. Rather, the average palace was constructed from mud bricks strengthened by wooden timbers. Both of these materials are highly perishable over time. So only scattered remnants of the palaces have survived. The rest of these once important structures have crumbled back into the earth from which they were made. Like so many other decaying vestiges of the ancient world, if not for the interest shown in excavating and preserving them since the 1800s, over time they would have disappeared without a trace.

Chapter Five

FENDING OFF
ENEMIES: FORTRESSES
AND FORTIFICATIONS

Some of the surviving fortresses of ancient Egypt are among the most impressive of that land's architectural and engineering achievements. Great tombs like the pyramids, giant statues like the Sphinx, and sacred shrines like Ramesses II's temple complex at Abu Simbel had no connection with war. And in examining them it is easy to forget that warfare, or at least the threat of attack, played a key role in the history and culture of ancient Egypt.

The need for particular kinds of fortifications, as perceived by the Egyptians themselves, grew mainly out of their country's unique geographical situation. Most of the populace lived in a narrow strip of land bordering the Nile. It ran north to south from the Nile Delta (on the Mediterranean coast) to Aswan, near the First Cataract. (Cataracts are places where

the river changes elevation, producing rapids.) Beyond this fertile band, with the exception of an occasional oasis, stretched many miles of arid deserts, creating a formidable natural barrier.

As a result, for a long time the populated portions of Egypt remained more or less isolated (as well as insulated) from the outside world. During and before the Old Kingdom (including the Predynastic Period, ca. 5500 to ca. 3100 B.C., and Early Dynastic Period, ca. 3100 to ca. 2686 B.C.), this gave the Egyptians an exaggerated sense of self-importance. They saw themselves as living in the center of creation. Indeed, their cherished religious ideology held that the world's first inhabitable land had appeared in their midst. The logical extension of this thinking was that the natural, cosmic order revolved around them and their culture. And outsiders—those

Ramesses III vs. the Sea Peoples

The fortresslike aspects of the Medinet Habu mortuary temple were strongly emphasized by Ramesses III when he adorned the place with relief sculptures that celebrated his great victory over the Sea Peoples. Scholar Manuel Robbins describes the scene depicted in the carving (in an excerpt from his book The Collapse of the Bronze Age *).*

The Sea Battle sculptural relief on the north wall of the temple is about 55 feet wide. . . . Here, represented in a compressed composition . . . was a clash which occurred on the water somewhere near shore. . . . On the right stands the pharaoh . . . launching shafts at the enemy from his unerring bow. Stretching across the bottom of the illustration are Egyptian soldiers, marching off with Sea Peoples prisoners. On the left is the battle on the water. . . . Here there is a clash among ships . . . [which] are arranged in three rows, one above the other. . . . The scene shows a fierce mêlée of close combat. Egyptian boats have their oars out so that they are able to maneuver, but in the Sea Peoples boats, oars are shipped [pulled inside the vessels]. They are unable to maneuver. They have been caught by surprise it seems. From a crow's nest on an Egyptian ship, a slinger rains missiles down on the Sea Peoples. A grappling hook has been swung out from an Egyptian ship and lands on a Sea Peoples ship. The ship is hauled close. . . . Another Sea Peoples ship is dismasted, a third capsized. Sea Peoples are in disarray, drowned, dead. The water is filled with them.

who lived on the "fringes" beyond Egypt's borders—were hostile, backward, evil, cowardly, and/or a perpetual threat to the cosmic order.

It was essential, therefore, to keep the unwanted outsiders out and to protect the nation and its people from danger and cultural pollution. Up until the start of the New Kingdom (in the 1500s B.C.), maintaining such defensive security was an accepted and expected part of each pharaoh's job. Fortresses and other kinds of fortifications were integral to these defenses and had two primary aims. The first was to guard and maintain the country's borders against possible threats. The other was to help exploit the natural resources, including building materials and local manpower, that existed on or slightly beyond those borders.

This basic strategy changed markedly with the advent of the New Kingdom. In the century preceding this period, an Asiatic people, the Hyksos, had occupied the country, fulfilling the Egyptians' worst fears of intrusion by outsiders. The Hyksos were eventually driven out. But in their wake they left the Egyptians with the disturbing feeling that their borders might never be completely secure. Their new strategy, one pursued by a series of vigorous warrior-kings, was to go beyond the borders and deliver preemptive strikes to any enemies that posed a potential threat. In this way, many of Egypt's forts became way stations on the road to conquest in an age of empire building.

Early Fortifications

Such attacks on foreign lands were definitely not part of the mindset and political policies of the earliest Egyptian leaders. The battles they fought and defenses they built were restricted mainly to the inhabited region of the Nile Valley. Before Egypt was a unified nation, it consisted of two kingdoms, one in the south (called Upper Egypt because it lay closer to the Nile's source), the other in the north (Lower Egypt). And scholars think these kingdoms coalesced from a number of smaller city-states that existed in the early fourth millennium B.C. Periodic fighting almost certainly occurred among these states and kingdoms. And each felt the need to erect fortifications to protect itself from aggressive neighbors.

The first-known examples of such fortifications in Egypt were the defensive walls of towns, a feature common to settlements and cities throughout ancient times in most parts of the world. A surviving fragment of a pottery model of a city wall, dated to the Predynastic Period, appears to depict two soldiers peering over a crenellated battlement. (In crenellation, stone notches alternate with open spaces, a familiar feature of castles in ancient and medieval times; bowmen and other soldiers hid behind the pro-

tective notches and discharged their weapons through the open spaces.) Such walls and battlements were originally constructed of mud bricks. Later, these were supplemented, especially around the gates, with blocks of sandstone and other kinds of stone. Whatever they were made of, such walls often reached heights of thirty to forty feet.

Egyptian leaders felt the need to continue building and maintaining such defensive walls, including the crenellated variety, after Upper and Lower Egypt came together to form the world's first major nation-state. This milestone occurred in about 3100 B.C., when Menes (also called Narmer), a king of Upper Egypt, conquered the rival kingdom and became the first pharaoh (as well as the first ruler of the First Dynasty). Either Menes,

The ruins at Buhen contain some of Egypt's best-preserved ancient fortifications.

or his son, Aha, established a new capital, Memphis (located about fifteen miles south of modern Cairo). Archaeologists have determined that the city was heavily fortified, a fact reflected in its earliest name—the White Wall.

It remains unclear whether the first pharaohs ever had to put Memphis's defenses to the test in actual warfare. But attacks and sieges of fortified towns did occur during the country's early history. During the civil conflicts of the unstable First Intermediate Period (ca. 2181–2055 B.C.), a number of towns with crenellated battlements underwent attack. Modern excavators have uncovered a mass grave at Deir el-Bahari (across the Nile from Thebes) near the base of such a battlement. The many cracked and dented skulls in the grave are those of troops who tried but failed either to breach or defend the walls.

Fortifying Temples

Towns were not the only human-made habitations or monuments that were fortified in Egypt's early centuries. Some temples also had tall defensive walls. Several of these were erected by the First Dynasty kings at Abydos (located on the Nile's west bank several miles northwest of Thebes). One temple, honoring Osiris, lord of the Underworld, was enclosed by two mud-brick walls. The inner one was almost forty feet high and nearly twenty feet wide at its base, while the outer wall stood about seventeen feet high. The two walls were separated from each other by about ten feet.

These structures are now badly eroded and decayed, and the reason they were fortified is not clear. It is possible that the temple enclosures doubled as forts to which the local natives retreated in times of danger. However, some scholars, including Egyptologist David O'Connor, think the walls had a more religious and symbolic value than a practical one. According to this view, these fortifications were intended to represent the so-called fortifications of the gods, which are mentioned in some early Egyptian inscriptions. Supposedly, certain gods periodically gathered in such enclosures to take part in various rituals. Therefore, the Abydos temples may have been fortified to curry favor with divine forces; and their use in repelling attackers may have been secondary.

The symbolic meaning of fortifying selected temples may or may not have carried over into later ages in Egypt. But there is no doubt that some temples in the New Kingdom possessed defenses designed to withstand real attacks, perhaps even full-fledged sieges. Medinet Habu, erected by Ramesses III, is the most obvious, as well as the best-preserved, example. Noted scholar Richard H. Wilkinson describes its imposing front section:

In ancient times Medinet Habu was fronted by an impressive landing quay at which the boats that came to the site via the canals which linked the temple to the Nile could moor. This quay stood before the main, eastern entrance to the complex—a large gateway of distinctive design modeled after a west-

The degree to which some temples were fortified can be seen in this view of one of the temples at Abydos.

ern Asiatic *migdol,* or fortress. Fronted by guardhouses, the sides of the gateway are decorated with images of the king trampling the enemies of Egypt.[39]

Among these enemies the pharaoh crushes are the so-called Sea Peoples. In the eighth year of Ramesses' reign (ca. 1174 B.C.), large groups of invaders (perhaps from a number of eastern Mediterranean locales) appeared in boats and attacked the Nile Delta. In one or more huge battles, Ramesses defeated them. The Medinet Habu complex was then under construction and was completed about four years later. It is possible, therefore, that fear of renewed attacks by the Sea Peoples (some of whom might conceivably have sailed

down the Nile and assaulted Thebes and other cities) may have partly motivated the unusually formidable defenses at Medinet Habu.

The Purposes of Frontier Fortresses

In addition to fortifying many towns and some temples, the Egyptians erected a number of military fortresses during the Old and Middle Kingdoms. These were located primarily along the frontiers between Egypt and foreign territories. The chief frontiers were those on the borders with Nubia (occupied mainly by black Africans), located in the south; Palestine, lying northeast of the Nile Delta and Sinai Peninsula; and

Capturing a Fortress by Trickery

Egyptian fortresses were designed to withstand direct frontal attacks. But sometimes the enemy found more subtle ways to get inside, including tricking the defenders into lowering their defenses. Perhaps the most famous Egyptian story of such a ruse tells how the pharaoh Thutmose III supposedly captured the city of Jaffa (in Palestine). The Egyptian commander, Thot, sent a message to the prince of Jaffa, saying that Thot had decided to surrender and would signify his submission by sending gifts in baskets. Thot sent two hundred baskets, inside each of which was a fully armed Egyptian soldier. Thinking that Thot was surrendering, the prince of Jaffa allowed him to enter the city accompanied by a number of unarmed men carrying the gift baskets. Once inside, these men unsealed the baskets, and the soldiers inside jumped out and captured the city.

Libya, situated due west of the delta. Ian Shaw elaborates in this excerpt from his book on Egyptian warfare:

The question of Egyptian fortresses . . . is very closely connected with that of the frontiers. The traditional borders of Egypt comprised the Western Desert, the Sinai Desert, the Mediterranean coast, and the First Nile Cataract at Aswan. . . . The northeastern, northwestern, and southern borders of Egypt were more or less fortified from the time of the Middle Kingdom onwards. From at least . . . 1962 B.C., the eastern Delta was protected by a string of fortresses, known as the Walls of the Prince. These were intended to prevent invasion along the coastal route from [Palestine]. . . . At about the same time, a fortress seems to have been established in the Wadi Natrun [an oasis situated several miles south of Alexandria], defending the western Delta from the Libyans. The western and eastern Delta defenses were well maintained throughout the second millennium B.C.[40]

During the Middle Kingdom, the perceived necessity for these outposts in the three main frontier areas was based on the traditional view that guarding the borders was integral to the safety and well-being of the nation. Later, in the New Kingdom, some of the Egyptian troops stationed in the fortresses continued to occupy them year round to maintain this defensive posture. But others were more mobile and went on the offensive; they left the fortresses and followed their pharaohs on military campaigns into foreign regions.

Of the three frontiers, the Nubian one features the best-preserved walls and fortresses. And studies show that their use and physical layout were probably fairly representative of examples elsewhere in

Egypt. The first permanently occupied fort in the Nubian frontier was built during the Old Kingdom. It was located at Buhen, near the Second Cataract, and consisted of a small settlement protected by a high, sturdy stone defensive wall.

Archaeologists have determined that those who occupied the enclosure at Buhen in the Old and Middle Kingdoms were mainly involved in copper smelting. This confirms that Egypt's primary interest in Nubia in those centuries was the exploitation of raw materials. Indeed, Egyptian military ventures into Nubia, which became considerably more frequent in the Middle Kingdom, were primarily motivated by the desire to maintain and protect the northward flow of valuable goods. To this end,

between about 1970 and 1840 B.C. a long chain of forts grew up between Aswan, near the First Cataract, and Buhen, near the Second Cataract. These functioned as customs stations as well as military outposts. They were a means to facilitate Egyptian traders entering and leaving Nubia while keeping most Nubian herders and traders from moving northward into Egypt. Part of the proof takes the form of a message carved on a stele erected in the frontier by the pharaoh Senusret III in about 1866 B.C.:

[The southern boundary of the realm is hereby marked] in order to prevent that any black Nubian should cross it, by water or by land, with a ship or any

Many of the defensive walls at Buhen are still intact. This photo shows their close proximity to the Nile.

herds [of livestock belonging to] the black Nubians, except a black Nubian ... with a commission [a written contract or permission slip from the Egyptian government]. Every good thing shall be done with them, but without allowing a ship of black Nubians to pass by Semna, going downstream forever. [41]

These forts continued to be used as customs stations in the New Kingdom. However, this role now clearly took second place to the military role. Numerous New Kingdom rulers led campaigns into Nubia, and the frontier fortresses became launching points for troops as well as storage facilities for essential weapons and supplies used in the campaigns. An inscription found at Aswan describes such a campaign by the pharaoh Thutmose II (reigned 1492–1479 B.C.):

> Then his majesty dispatched a numerous army into Nubia on his first occasion of a campaign, in order to overthrow all those who were rebellious against his majesty or hostile to the Lord of the Two Lands [i.e., Egypt]. Then this army of his majesty overthrew those barbarians; they did not let live anyone among their males, according to all the command of his majesty, except one of those children of the chief of wretched Nubia, who was taken away alive as a living prisoner with their people to his majesty.... This land was made a subject of his majesty as formerly, [and]

the people rejoiced [and] the chiefs were joyful. [42]

The Command Structure and Layout of Forts

The pharaoh himself was usually in direct charge of such operations and commanded a fortress during the short time he stayed in one on his way to engage the enemy. The rest of the time, the commander of the installation was an official known as a fort officer. His military rank seems to have been roughly equal to the commander of a host, an army unit made up of five hundred men. (That does not necessarily mean that every fort was garrisoned by five hundred troops.) Evidence suggests that a fort officer reported directly to the pharaoh's vizier, the kingdom's chief administrative official after the pharaoh himself. The second in command of a fort was an officer with the title "scribe of the fort." The fact that he was a scribe suggests that he was in charge of duty rosters and kept careful records of incoming and outgoing troops and supplies.

The basic ground plans of the fortresses these officers oversaw were all fairly similar. Each consisted of a well-organized grid of narrow streets lined with storerooms, workshops, barracks for the soldiers, and larger quarters for the officers. A wider street encircled the complex on the inside of the defensive wall, allowing the residents easy access to the battlements in an emergency. Most of the forts were erected near the Nile and had protected walkways or tunnels leading to the river to ensure an

A computerized reconstruction of the Buhen fortress on the banks of the Nile shows high defensive walls surrounding an inner village.

ample supply of fresh water in case of a siege.

The defensive walls that surrounded the inner structures and streets of a fortress complex were tall, imposing, and, not surprisingly, designed to repel large-scale attacks. The best-preserved example, at Buhen, featured especially impressive walls and battlements. They "comprise four basic elements," writes Yigael Yadin, a noted expert on ancient Near Eastern warfare,

the main (inner) wall, the outer or advance wall, the moat, and the very well-fortified gate structure. The main wall was built of bricks and was about five meters [16 feet] thick. It is considered [by experts] to have been 10 meters [33 feet] high. The gate was in the center of the western side of the wall. Throughout its entire length, the wall was "blistered" at intervals of 5 meters with protruding square bastions [large stone barriers], each two meters [6.5 feet] wide. Each corner of the fortress was marked by a large tower, which protruded from the face of the wall even more conspicuously than the bastions. An impressive feature of the Buhen fortifications is the [positioning] and the form of the low outer wall. . . . This low wall was also of brick, and along its face a series of semicircular bastions 3 meters [10 feet] wide had been built at intervals of 10 meters. In the wall and the bastion were two rows of firing [holes]. . . . Each enabled fire [the release of arrows and other missile weapons] to be applied downward onto the attackers in the moat in three directions. . . . At the foot of the outer wall there was a dry moat 8.5 meters [28 feet] wide and more than 6 meters [20 feet] deep. To make it even more difficult to cross, an additional low wall had been built on its farther bank.[43]

One of the more revealing features of the Buhen fortress is the gate complex because it demonstrates that the Egyptians had a fairly sophisticated grasp of the art of defensive fortification. A tower similar to those situated at the corners of the fortress stood on each side of the large, double-doored gate. These gate towers extended outward for forty-nine feet, well past the low wall on the outer bank of the moat. Defenders could stand on a crenellated walkway at the top of these towers, so that they overlooked and could fire weapons down onto the area directly in front of the gate. This suggests that would-be attackers had and could be expected to use battering rams designed to crash through the gates.

Besieging Fortified Places

These descriptions of the defenses possessed by the fortresses and the offensive devices employed against them by attackers lead inevitably to the topic of sieges. Whether it was enemy troops attacking an Egyptian fortress or Egyptian troops attacking a fortified enemy town, sieges were an inevitable fact of life in Egypt and surrounding regions, especially during the

New Kingdom. Both defensive and offensive siege operations were characterized by the military technology and methods then available. And the tactics of attack and defense played off of and stimulated each other. In other words, when someone invented a new siege engine capable of damaging a fortress, the defenders rapidly devised a counterdevice or counterstrategy to meet the threat. Soon the besiegers introduced another innovation, the defenders countered it, and so it went. In this way, "fortifications and siege warfare are inextricably [inescapably] combined," noted scholar Peter Connolly writes. "The development of one inevitably stimulates changes in the other,"[44] and therefore the two must be considered together.

As for the offensive tactics and devices that fortresses, as well as town defensive walls, attempted to counter, some descriptions of them have survived in written accounts, paintings, and sculptures. An instructive example consists of the tactics employed in the siege of Megiddo (in Palestine), prosecuted by Thutmose III in about the year 1482 B.C. According to that pharaoh's official annals:

His majesty commanded the officers of the troops to go [forth and besiege the citadel], assigning to each his place. They measured this city, surrounding it with an enclosure, walled about with green timber of all their pleasant trees. His majesty himself was upon the fortification east of this city, inspecting [the work].... It was walled about with a thick wall.... Its name was made:

"Thutmose III-is-the-Surrounder-of-the-Asiatics." People were stationed to watch over the tent of his majesty, to whom it was said: "Steady of heart!" His majesty commanded [his men], saying "Let not one among them [the confined enemy] come forth outside, beyond this wall, except to come out in order to knock at the door of their fortification [i.e., to signal that they are ready to surrender the city]."[45]

As this account suggests, the enclosure wall Thutmose built around the city was intended to prevent any of the defenders from escaping and also to keep food and/or reinforcements from getting in. Another revealing point is that the wall was made by using wood from "all" the trees in the area. Eliminating any forests around a fortress or town not only provided plenty of material for the offensive enclosure wall but also removed hiding places for anyone who might manage to escape from the besieged place. That this was a common technique in sieges during the New Kingdom is proven by a passage from the biblical book of Deuteronomy, written during that era. The passage advises attackers to cut down the surrounding trees, except for fruit trees, which would be valuable to them as a food source.

The carved reliefs commissioned by other pharaohs illustrate other common siege tactics and devices used against fortresses. A relief found in a tomb at a burial site near Memphis shows an army of Egyptians besieging an enemy fortress. Some of the soldiers are in the process of digging a sap (tunnel) under the walls. A sap either weakened the walls, causing them to collapse, or gave the attackers access to the citadel, or both. As the sappers work (in the relief), other Egyptians

Biblical Advice on Prosecuting a Siege

The surviving information for ancient Egyptian fortresses, fortification walls, and sieges comes from a variety of sources. Some, of course, take the form of the ruins of the walls and fortresses themselves. There are also a few relief sculptures showing armies attacking fortresses. In addition, there are scattered written accounts, some from Egypt, others from neighboring lands. The biblical book of Deuteronomy is one of the latter. It was composed by Jews in Palestine in the later years of the Egyptian period now called the New Kingdom, and the following excerpt advises attackers on which trees to cut down during the prosecution of a siege: "When you besiege a city for a long time, making war against it in order to take it . . . only the trees which you know are not trees for food you may destroy and cut down that you may build siege works against the city that makes war with you, until it falls."

The looming figure of Thutmose III dwarfs those of his many war captives in this relief from the Karnak complex.

climb scaling ladders that lean against the fortress walls. The ladders have wheels at the bottom, indicating that they have been rolled rather than carried into place. The evidence is clear that, as the Egyptians climbed the ladders, the defenders tried to push the ladders away. At the same time, Egyptian bowmen fired arrows at the battlements to provide cover for their comrades climbing the ladders. Other reliefs show attackers using battle axes to chop down fortress gates, which were made of wood.

The fortresses and other fortifications the Egyptians built had to be large and strong in order to withstand such vigorous attacks. This shows that the Egyptians could produce monumental architecture that was quite practical, along with structures fulfilling religious and artistic needs and expression. A pyramid, for example, possessed great religious and mystical significance; but it was not very practical. In contrast, all of the energies funneled into building a fortress or a defensive wall had an obvious and often fairly immediate payoff—the survival of the nation and its people.

Chapter Six

WONDER OF THE WORLD: ALEXANDRIA'S GREAT LIGHTHOUSE

I n the second century B.C. a Greek traveler and writer named Antipater of Sidon compiled a now famous list of what he viewed as the seven structures that most deserved to be called "wonders of the world." The oldest and certainly the largest of these consisted of Khufu's great pyramid at Giza. Antipater's list also included another Egyptian monument—the towering lighthouse at Alexandria (on the Mediterranean coast in the western Nile Delta). As near as modern scholars can tell, it was the world's first formal lighthouse; and it became the prototype, or model, for nearly all other lighthouses subsequently erected across the ancient Mediterranean world. In the first century A.D., Pliny the

Elder wrote, "Similar beacons [patterned after it] now burn brightly in several places, for example at Ostia [Rome's port] and Ravenna [in northeastern Italy]." [46]

Pliny also addressed the needs fulfilled by the great Alexandrian structure. "Its purpose," he said, "is to provide a beacon for ships sailing by night, to warn them of shallows, and to mark the entrance to the harbor." [47] The latter reason listed by Pliny—to show mariners where Alexandria's harbor lay, even in the daytime—was perhaps the most important. The Egyptian coastline in this region was very flat and devoid of prominent landmarks, which made it difficult for ancient sailors to sight the exact location of the city from miles out at sea.

The Seven Wonders of the World

In about 130 B.C. a Greek writer and traveler named Antipater of Sidon compiled a list of what he saw as the seven great architectural wonders of his world. In addition to the Pharos at Alexandria, they included the Great Pyramid of Khufu at Giza, built more than two thousand years before Antipater's era; the Hanging Gardens of Babylon, a series of gardens built on terraces in the royal palace of a Babylonian king during the sixth century B.C.; the gigantic Greek temple at Ephesus, located on the Aegean coast of Asia Minor, dedicated to Artemis (a goddess who protected animals); the giant statue of the god Zeus that rested in his temple at Olympia in southern Greece; the Mausoleum at Halicarnassus, near Ephesus, a magnificently decorated tomb built for a local king, Mausolus, by his wife; and the Colossus of Rhodes, a giant statue of the Sun god, Helios, erected on the Greek island of Rhodes to celebrate its survival following a long siege.

This colored engraving is based on a nineteenth-century drawing of the Hanging Gardens of Babylon, erected in the sixth century B.C.

The first-century A.D. Jewish historian Josephus added these facts: "It is difficult even in peacetime for ships to approach the harbor of Alexandria; the entrance is narrow, and submerged rocks make a straight course impossible. The left side is shut in by artificial moles [mounds of rocks and earth]."[48] For these reasons the builders situated the great lighthouse in a central position, on Pharos Island, near the entrance to the main harbor (the eastern one, which housed the royal fleets). The building subsequently became so closely associated with this small island that the structure itself became known as the "Pharos" of Alexandria (or of Egypt).

The fact that the Pharos was built in Alexandria highlights an important difference between it and the pyramids, the Great Sphinx, and the temples and colossi of Ramesses II and other rulers of the Old, Middle, and New Kingdoms. These other, more ancient monuments were sponsored, designed, and built by native Egyptians. In contrast, the Pharos was financed and designed by Greeks, although most of the laborers were likely native Egyptians. The story of how the Greeks established themselves in Egypt and built Alexandria and its many famous structures, including the Pharos, constitutes part of the fascinating background history of that great wonder of the ancient world.

Homer Lures the Greeks to Pharos Island

By the time work began on the towering lighthouse at Alexandria, the great ages of native Egyptian warrior- and builder-pharaohs were a distant memory. In about the year 1069 B.C., the glorious New Kingdom, in which Egypt had reached its height of power and influence, ended. And thereafter, the country continued in a political and military decline that had begun under the last few New Kingdom pharaohs. Beginning in the eighth century B.C. a series of foreign rulers took the Egyptian throne, including Nubians and Persians.

Egypt languished under Persian rule for two centuries. Then the Macedonian Greek king and military adventurer Alexander III (later called "the Great") invaded the Persian Empire (in 334 B.C.) and rapidly brought it to its knees. In 332 Alexander entered Egypt, ending Persian rule there. The Egyptians did not regain their independence, however, for Alexander merely substituted his own power for that of the Persian monarchs. He, a Greek, was for all intents and purposes the new pharaoh and had total control of the country.

Alexander stayed only a few months in Egypt before continuing with his conquest of Persia. In that short span, however, he accomplished something that was destined to have a tremendous impact on the future of Egypt and of the Mediterranean world in general; namely, he established a new Egyptian capital city, naming it Alexandria after himself. His first order of business was to choose a site. And he hoped to find a suitable spot on the Mediterranean coast, which would be more accessible to shipping and trade than the old inland capitals of Memphis and Thebes. Alexander remembered a passage from the *Odyssey,* one of the great

This illustration depicts Alexander and his architect laying out the street grid for the new city of Alexandria.

literary epics by the renowned Greek poet Homer. In this tract, Homer had described an island off Egypt's coast, one that even Alexander could not foresee would one day be the location of a great wonder of the world. "There is an island called Pharos in the rolling seas off the mouth of the Nile," the passage begins,

> a day's sail out for a well-found vessel with a roaring wind astern. In this island is a sheltered cove where sailors come to draw their water from a well and can launch their boats on an even keel into the deep sea. It was here that the gods kept me idle for twenty days; and all that time there was never a sign on the water of the steady breeze that ships require for a cruise across the open sea. . . . [Luckily, a goddess appeared and said,] "Sir, I will tell you all you need to know. This island is the haunt of that immortal seer, Proteus of Egypt, the Old Man of the Sea, who owes allegiance to [the Greek sea god] Poseidon and knows the sea in all its depths. He is my father too. . . . If you could contrive somehow to set a trap and catch him, he would tell you about your journey and the distances to be covered, and direct you home along the highways of the fish. [49]

Alexander's instincts told him that the place Homer had described might be the ideal spot to build his new city. To make sure, he immediately traveled there and surveyed the site. And he was not disappointed. According to the first-century A.D. Greek writer Plutarch, who wrote a biography of Alexander:

> When he saw what wonderful natural advantages the place possessed—for it was a strip of land resembling a broad isthmus which stretched between the sea and a great lagoon [Lake Mareotis], with a spacious harbor at the end of it—he declared that Homer, besides his other admirable qualities, was also a far-seeing architect, and he ordered the plan of the city to be designed so that it would conform to this site. [50]

Alexandria subsequently became a great cosmopolitan city, one of the three largest and most prosperous in the Western world (along with Rome, Italy, and Antioch, Syria). Alexander did not live to see it completed, however. He died in 323 B.C., shortly after completing his conquest of Persia. The Egyptian throne then fell to one of his leading generals, a Macedonian aristocrat named Ptolemy (pronounced TAW-luh-mee), who established a new dynasty and thereby initiated the Greek, or Ptolemaic, Period of ancient Egypt.

Who Built the Pharos?

After declaring himself king of Egypt, Ptolemy took the title of Ptolemy I Soter (*Soter* means "Savior"). He and his son, Ptolemy II Philadelphus, erected many fine buildings and made Alexandria a showplace for locals and foreign visitors alike. Among these structures were huge palaces, beautiful temples, a university-like institution called the Museum, and the Great Library, which came to house the largest collection of books in the ancient world.

A human hero wrestles with the mythical Proteus on Pharos Island.

An ancient coin bears the likeness of Ptolemy I, who began the Pharos.

three centuries after the fact. His assertion that the pharaoh allowed Sostratos to inscribe his own name in a spirit of generosity may have been an assumption designed to explain the unusual deviation from normal practice.

It is possible, therefore, that there was no deviation from normal practice and that Sostratos himself paid most or all of the costs of erecting the Pharos. It does seem improbable that an architect, in those days a mere artisan, would be rich enough to finance such an enormous construction project. So it is possible that this Sostratos was not the famous architect Sostratos of Cnidus but rather a wealthy Greek who was his son, grandson, or nephew. Because they shared the same name, writers in later generations might have mistaken one for the other.

The truth will likely never be known, partly because a famous story connected with the dedication of the lighthouse could be used to support either theory. According to this tale, Ptolemy II forbade Sostratos (either as financier or architect) from carving his own name on the monument. But Sostratos made sure that posterity would not forget his contribution. According to the second-century A.D. Greek writer Lucian, he carved a message on the foundation stone stating that he, Sostratos, dedicated the lighthouse to the "Savior Gods" on behalf of sailors and seafarers. Then Sostratos covered the message with plaster; when it dried, he carved

The great lighthouse on Pharos Island was another noteworthy achievement of their reigns. It remains unclear, however, if the first two Ptolemies actually financed the monument, or at least whether they did so alone. Pliny said that "King Ptolemy [in this case Ptolemy II], in a spirit of generosity, allowed the name of the architect, Sostratos of Cnidus, to be inscribed on the building itself."[51] This suggests that the king paid for the lighthouse and the architect put his name on the foundation stone. The problem is that in ancient times it was the universal custom for the person who financed a building to put his or her name on it. Remember that Pliny was writing some

A Greek Writer Describes Alexandria

In this excerpt from volume 8 of his Library of History, *the first-century B.C. Greek historian Diodorus Siculus describes Alexandria's general layout as it appeared in his day.*

[A]lexander] gave orders to . . . build the city between the marsh [Lake Mareotis] and the sea. He laid out the site and traced the streets skillfully. . . . By selecting the right angle of the streets, Alexander made the city breathe with the etesian winds, so that as these blow across a great expanse of sea, they cool the air of the town, and so he provided its inhabitants with a moderate climate and good health.

Alexander also laid out the walls so that they were at once exceedingly large and marvelously strong. . . . In shape, it [the city] is similar to a *chlamys* [a cloak commonly worn by soldiers and young men], and it is approximately bisected by an avenue remarkable for its size and beauty. From gate to gate it [the avenue] runs a distance of [nearly five miles]; it is [100 feet] in width, and is bordered throughout its length with rich façades of houses and temples. . . . The city in general has grown so much in later times that many reckon it to be the first city of the civilized world, and it is certainly far ahead of all the rest in elegance and extent [size] and riches and luxury.

Alexandria, part of which is reconstructed in this modern woodcut, was one of the world's great cities.

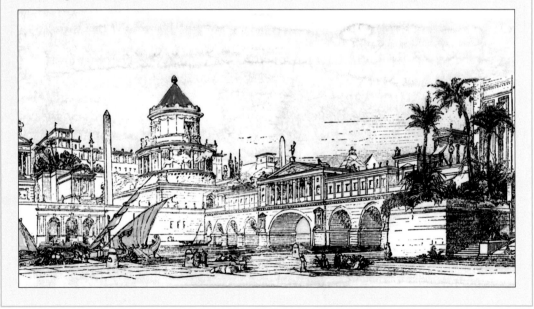

into it the dedication to the pharaoh that Ptolemy had demanded. The years and centuries passed. And rain and wind wore away the plaster, erasing the king's name and leaving Sostratos's, which was still plainly visible in Pliny's and Lucian's eras.

There is no way to know if this story is true or a mere fable. But Lucian was not the only ancient writer who claimed to have seen such words carved at the base of the Pharos. The first-century B.C. Greek geographer Strabo, a highly reputable source, was another. Assuming the story was true, what did Sostratos mean by the "Savior Gods," to whom he dedicated the lighthouse? Some scholars think he was referring to Ptolemy I and his queen, Berenice, since the first Ptolemy took the title of "Savior." Another theory is that the Savior Gods were the mythical characters Castor and Pollux, who came to be seen as patron gods of navigators and rescuers of drowning sailors. Still another view, perhaps the most widely accepted, is that Sostratos was referring to Proteus, the sea god whom Homer said made his home on Pharos Island, and Zeus, leader of the Greek gods. This theory is strengthened by the fact that a statue of Zeus Soter ("Zeus the Savior") did stand at the pinnacle of the completed Pharos.

Whoever financed the great lighthouse, he had to have been very well off. Pliny, among others, asserted that it cost eight hundred talents to construct. In ancient times, a talent was a mass of silver weighing roughly fifty-seven to fifty-eight pounds. Based on the average market price of silver in U.S. dollars in 2004, the Pharos cost the equivalent of approximately $470 million in modern money.

The Pharos's Door and Lower Level

What did this very expensive, impressive, and renowned lighthouse look like? Unfortunately, the accounts of the Greek and Roman authors are not very helpful in this regard. Pliny gave no specific description of the monument. And though Strabo described Pharos Island in fair detail, he said only the following about the lighthouse: "[It is] a tower that is admirably constructed of white marble with many stories and bears the same name as the island." [52]

Fortunately for posterity, long after Greco-Roman civilization passed away a medieval Arab traveler provided the most comprehensive written description of the Pharos. In 1166 Abou Haggag el-Andaloussi visited Alexandria and made a detailed examination of the old lighthouse. From his account, modern scholars have gained a fairly reliable picture of what it looked like.

El-Andaloussi began with a few general remarks about the island, which he said was uninhabited, and the great monument, which was still largely intact after more than fourteen centuries. "The Pharos rises at the end of the island," el-Andaloussi said.

The building is square. . . . The sea surrounds the Pharos except on the east and south sides. . . . It is strongly built, the stones being well shaped and laid and long with a rougher finish than elsewhere on the building. . . . On the seaward wall, that is the south side, there is an ancient inscription which I cannot read. . . . The combination of the sea and the air has worn away the background stone and the letters stand out in relief because of their hardness. . . . The doorway to the Pharos is high up. A ramp . . . used to lead up to it. This ramp rests on a series of curved arches. . . . There are sixteen of these arches each gradually getting higher until the doorway is reached.[53]

El-Andaloussi (accompanied by a few companions) entered this door and made his way into the lighthouse. He explored the entire structure and made careful measurements of the various sections. His account, supplemented by images of the Pharos on ancient coins, guides the following reconstruction of the various levels, stairways, and chambers.

The Pharos consisted of three main sections, one resting atop another. The lowest and most massive section was about 197 feet, or eighteen stories, in height and was square in shape. This lower level contained many dozens of rooms, most of which el-Andaloussi and his companions examined. "We entered and found ourselves in a room," he wrote, "followed by another and others just the same for a total of 18 rooms along a corridor." More corridors and rooms led off of a "ramp that gradually ascended around the cylindrical core of this huge building."[54]

Modern archaeologists and architects have speculated about these interior features of the lighthouse's lower level. The numerous chambers may have had various functions. Some may have served as living quarters for the workers who staffed the facility. Other rooms were likely used to store the wood and/or other materials that fueled the fire that burned at the top of the structure. The "cylindrical core" mentioned by el-Andaloussi was almost certainly a thick and sturdy stone construction designed to carry the enormous weight of the upper levels of the building.

This drawing provides a fair approximation of how the completed Pharos appeared.

The Lighthouse's Upper Stories

Reaching the top of the first level, el-Andaloussi and his assistants found a flat platform that wound around the base of the building's second level. In ancient times, when the lighthouse was in its prime, this was likely an observation deck. Guides probably allowed tourists to stop here and gaze out at Alexandria's wide avenues and splendid monuments.

The second level, said el-Andaloussi, was not square shaped but rather "in the shape of an octagon [an eight-sided figure]."[55] It was about ninety-eight feet high, and its interior had a staircase rather than a ramp. The staircase wound around the inner core, and the outer wall featured small windows placed at intervals of about ten feet.

On top of the second level was another observation deck, which surrounded the base of the third and final level. This upper section was cylindrical (round) in shape and

The Pharos's Image on Coins

Images of the great lighthouse at Alexandria appeared on numerous coins issued in ancient times. Among the best preserved are some from Egypt's Roman period (30 B.C.–A.D. 395), made in Alexandria, which housed one of the Roman Empire's major coin mints. In his book about the seven wonders of the ancient world (written with Martin Price), scholar Peter Clayton describes the images on some of these coins.

The basic form of the representation of the Pharos [on coins] was always the same . . . and there is a greater amount of accuracy in them than is often given credit. On the coin representations of the Pharos up to and including the reign of [the Roman emperor] Hadrian [in the early second century A.D.], the entrance doorway is seen either at ground level or at least placed very low on the building. . . . [Another coin] shows a particularly fine and clear representation of the Pharos with circular windows on the tall first stage and Tritons [statues of minor sea gods] blowing their trumpets hanging off the upper edges . . . and two very truncated second and third stages, the upper topped by the statue of Zeus Soter. . . . [Another coin] shows it [the lighthouse] with a [ship] sailing past.

A Roman coin shows a ship approaching the Pharos.

about twenty-six feet high. At its summit, el-Andaloussi and the others found a small Muslim mosque, which had been added sometime in the preceding few centuries.

In ancient times, however, the space occupied by the mosque was the area where attendants maintained the fire that constituted the lighthouse's famous beacon for sailors. Most scholars presume that a large curved mirror (made of polished copper or bronze) amplified the fire's light; although no direct evidence for such a mirror has yet been found. It has also been long assumed that the fire was fueled by wood. However, Egypt was at the time (and still is) largely devoid of forests, which raises the question of where the large quantities of wood needed to keep the fire going came from. Perhaps the wood was imported (at great expense) from neighboring lands; or maybe animal dung or some other fuel was used instead. For the moment, this aspect of the Pharos's operation remains unexplained.

The fire area atop the third level was surrounded by a circle of tall pillars, perhaps about fifteen feet high. The pillars supported a small cone-shaped roof on top of which the statue of Zeus Soter stood. Some evidence suggests that the statue was at least 15 feet high. That means that the heights of the various sections of the building were (going from top to bottom): 15 feet, 15 feet, 26 feet, 98 feet, and 197 feet. We must also add in another roughly 35 feet, the height above sea level at which the lighthouse's lowest level stood. That gives a total height of about 386 feet above sea level—approximately equivalent to a modern thirty-eight-to-thirty-nine-story skyscraper.

The fire atop the lighthouse created a beacon visible over great distances.

The great height of the Pharos ensured that the light it emitted was visible far out at sea. Exactly how far out is unknown and was a matter of dispute even in ancient times. Josephus wrote that the fires of the "enormous lighthouse" were "visible thirty-five miles away, warning visiting ships to anchor at night well away from the shore because of the difficulty of making the port."[56] In contrast, Lucian claimed that mariners could see the Pharos's beacon as far away as three hundred miles. Modern scholars think that Josephus's figure is more realistic. It is highly unlikely that the light of a bonfire, even a big one, would be visible for hundreds of miles.

The Pharos's Fate

One thing that nearly all the ancient writers who mentioned the Pharos agreed on was that it was very large, solid, and sturdy. Not surprisingly, that increased its chances for survival. And indeed, compared to most other ancient structures, the Pharos did remain intact for a long time—a total of nearly sixteen centuries. Scholars know this thanks to the survival of a number of ancient and medieval documents, coins, and pictorial representations mentioning or depicting the monument.

For example, a mosaic created in about 1200 proves that the lighthouse was still standing at that time. The mosaic, located on the ceiling of a chapel in St. Mark's Cathedral in Venice, Italy, shows the famous saint in a boat approaching Alexandria, where he went on to establish the Egyptian Christian (or Coptic) Church. Prominent in the right portion of the mosaic is the Pharos. It is almost certain that the artist worked from sketches or verbal descriptions supplied by someone who had personally seen the structure. The picture accurately shows its three levels, each smaller than the one below it, and the observation platforms atop the first and second levels. It also shows the small domed mosque mentioned by el-Andaloussi, who had visited the lighthouse fewer than forty years before the creation of the mosaic. Both el-Andaloussi's account and the Venice mosaic seem to confirm that the Pharos was still largely intact in the late twelfth century.

However, the evidence shows that at this point the great monument's days were numbered. Periodic earthquakes had weakened the Pharos over the centuries. And one or more unusually strong ones in the thirteenth and early fourteenth centuries apparently brought it down. In 1326 another Muslim traveler, Ibn Battuta, visited Alexandria and later reported that the upper portions of the building had collapsed. This was confirmed by a manuscript from the monastery at Montpellier, France, which reported that the Pharos fell during an earthquake that struck Egypt in August 1303.

Thereafter, the deterioration of the lighthouse's ruins was rapid. When Battuta paid a second visit to the site in 1349, he found that further collapse, accompanied by erosion from sea waves and the weather, had made it impossible to reach and enter the elevated main door. At the time, Egypt was controlled by Turkish rulers known as the Mamelukes. For a while they left the ruins of the Pharos alone. But in 1480 one of these sultans, Kait Bey, who feared attacks by another Turkish group, the Ottomans, decided to erect a fortress on the site. His builders utilized many of the stones from the fallen lighthouse. Though damaged when a British fleet bombarded it in 1882, the fortress was repaired and still stands. So today a few remnants of the Pharos remain on the spot where the lighthouse originally stood.

As for the rest of the pieces of the ancient monument, some were likely carted away for use in other newer buildings in Alexandria. The rest lie on the sea bottom near the shores of Pharos Island. In the 1960s an Egyptian diver discovered several stone blocks and statues that had once been part of the lighthouse. Since that time, French archaeologists have explored the nearby seabed and found more statues that likely stood beside the great monument in ancient times. (These scholars think that among the statues were colossi of some of the early Ptolemaic rulers.)

History's Ultimate Lesson

Study of these fascinating ancient artifacts is ongoing. At the same time, archaeologists continue to search for more remnants of the great lighthouse as well as temples, palaces, forts, tombs, and other great monuments

The fortress of Kait Bey rests on the original site of the Pharos and utilizes numerous stone blocks from the older monument.

erected by the ancient Egyptians. In their endeavors, these investigators of one of the world's great past cultures invariably gain a hearty respect for the ingenuity and determination of the ancient builders.

They also learn to view their own modern culture with a certain degree of humility. The people who raised the pyramids at Giza, the temples at Karnak, and the lighthouse at Alexandria believed that these structures would be maintained practically forever. And like people in every age and place, they could not conceive that their civilization would someday consist only of scattered ruins and dim memories. As Peter Clayton and Martin Price put it, "It is difficult at any time [in history] to realize that buildings with which people are familiar will be destroyed and that the civilization we know will be changed beyond all recognition."[57] Yet it is inevitable that the present civilization's fate will, sooner or later, be the same as that of the Egyptian builders and their once mighty works. This is the ultimate lesson of these monuments, and of history in general.

Notes

Introduction: The Labor of Forgotten Millions

1. Quoted in *Egypt: Yesterday and Today;* Lithographs by David Roberts; Text by Fabio Bourbon. New York: Stewarts Tabori, and Chang, 1996, p. 140.
2. Dieter Arnold, *Building in Egypt: Pharaonic Stone Masonry.* Oxford, UK: Oxford University Press, 1991, p. 4.
3. Herodotus, *The Histories,* trans. Aubrey de Sélincourt. New York: Penguin, 1972, pp. 178–79.
4. Kevin Jackson and Jonathan Stamp, *Building the Great Pyramid.* Toronto: Firefly, 2003, p. 32.
5. Eugen Strouhal, *Life of the Ancient Egyptians.* Norman: University of Oklahoma Press, 1992, p. 184.

Chapter One: Pyramids: Cutting, Lifting, and Setting the Stones

6. Kate Spence, "The Great Sphinx at Giza," in *The Seventy Wonders of the Ancient World,* ed. Chris Scarre. London: Thames and Hudson, 1999, p. 259.
7. Arnold, *Building in Egypt,* pp. 45, 257.
8. Jackson and Stamp, *Building the Great Pyramid,* p. 27.

9. Jackson and Stamp, *Building the Great Pyramid,* p. 66.
10. Kate Spence, "The Pyramids of Giza," in Scarre, ed., *Seventy Wonders of the Ancient World,* p. 25.
11. Jackson and Stamp, *Building the Great Pyramid,* p. 58.
12. Zahi Hawass, "The Discovery of the Tombs of the Pyramid Builders at Giza." www.guardians.net/hawass/buildtomb.htm.
13. Zahi Hawass, "Tombs of the Pyramid Builders," *Archaeology,* January/February 1997, pp. 39–43.

Chapter Two: Pyramids: Chambers, Security, and Mystical Elements

14. Herodotus, *Histories,* p. 143.
15. I.E.S. Edwards, *The Pyramids of Egypt.* New York: Penguin, 1993, p. 234.
16. Quoted in Josephine Mayer and Tom Prideaux, eds., *Never to Die: The Egyptians in Their Own Words.* New York: Viking, 1938, pp. 43–44.
17. Jackson and Stamp, *Building the Great Pyramid,* p. 29.
18. Spence, "The Pyramids of Giza," in Scarre, ed., *The Seventy Wonders of the Ancient World,* p. 24.
19. Jackson and Stamp, *Building the Great Pyramid,* p. 72.

20. Edwards, *The Pyramids of Egypt*, p. 226.
21. Peter Clayton and Martin Price, *The Seven Wonders of the Ancient World*. New York: Barnes and Noble, 1993, p. 30.
22. Quoted in Hawass, "The Discovery of the Tombs of the Pyramid Builders."
23. Clayton and Price, *The Seven Wonders of the Ancient World*, p. 30.
24. Ecclesiastes 9:11.

Chapter Three: The Colossi: The Sphinx and Other Giant Statues

25. Gay Robins, *Egyptian Statues*. Buckinghamshire, UK: Shire, 2003, p. 7.
26. Robins, *Egyptian Statues*, pp. 9–10.
27. Desmond Stewart, *The Pyramids and the Sphinx*. New York: Newsweek Book Division, 1971, p. 44.
28. Spence, "The Great Sphinx at Giza," in Scarre, ed., *The Seventy Wonders of the Ancient World*, p. 260.
29. Percy Bysshe Shelley, "Ozymandias," first published January 11, 1818, in the *Examiner*, no. 524. The poem can be found in thousands of books and Internet sites (in the latter by typing its title into a search engine).
30. Arnold, *Building in Egypt*, p. 231.
31. Shelley, "Ozymandias."

Chapter Four: Ties to the Divine: Temples, Obelisks, and Palaces

32. Kate Spence, "The Temples of Karnak," in Scarre, ed., *The Seventy Wonders of the Ancient World*, pp. 100–101.

33. Quoted in J.H. Breasted, ed., *Ancient Records of Egypt*, vol. 2. New York: Russell and Russell, 1962, pp. 190–91.
34. Steven Snape, *Egyptian Temples*. Buckinghamshire, UK: Shire, 1999, p. 29.
35. Zahi Hawass, *The Mysteries of Abu Simbel: Ramesses II and the Temples of the Rising Sun*. Cairo: American University in Cairo Press, 2001, pp. 69, 72, 76–77.
36. Arnold, *Building in Egypt*, p. 113.
37. Pliny the Elder, *Natural History*, in *Natural History: A Selection*, trans. John F. Healy. New York: Penguin, 1991, p. 350.
38. Ian Shaw and Paul Nicholson, *The Dictionary of Ancient Egypt*. New York: Harry N. Abrams, 1995, p. 217.

Chapter Five: Fending Off Enemies: Fortresses and Fortifications

39. Richard H. Wilkinson, *The Complete Temples of Ancient Egypt*. London: Thames and Hudson, 2000, p. 194.
40. Ian Shaw, *Egyptian Warfare and Weapons*. Buckinghamshire, UK: Shire, 1991, pp. 15–17.
41. Quoted in Breasted, *Ancient Records of Egypt*, vol. 1, pp. 293–94.
42. Quoted in Breasted, *Ancient Records of Egypt*, vol. 2, p. 50.
43. Yigael Yadin, *The Art of Warfare in Biblical Lands in the Light of Archaeological Study*, vol. 1. New York: McGraw-Hill, 1963, p. 66.

44. Peter Connolly, *Greece and Rome at War*. London: Greenhill, 1998, p. 274.

45. Quoted in Breasted, *Ancient Records of Egypt*, vol. 2, pp. 185–86.

Chapter Six: Wonder of the World: Alexandria's Great Lighthouse

46. Pliny the Elder, *Natural History*, p. 353.

47. Pliny the Elder, *Natural History*, p. 353.

48. Josephus, *The Jewish Wars*, trans. G.A. Williamson, rev. E. Mary Smallwood. New York: Penguin, 1981, p. 282.

49. Homer, *Odyssey*, trans. E.V. Rieu. Baltimore: Penguin, 1961, pp. 73–74.

50. Plutarch, *Life of Alexander*, in *The Age of Alexander: Nine Greek Lives by Plutarch*, trans. Ian Scott-Kilvert. New York: Penguin, 1973, pp. 281–82.

51. Pliny the Elder, *Natural History*, p. 353.

52. Strabo, *Geography*, vol. 8, trans. Horace L. Jones. Cambridge, MA: Harvard University Press, 1964, p. 63.

53. Quoted in Clayton and Price, *The Seven Wonders of the Ancient World*, pp. 153–54.

54. Quoted in Clayton and Price, *The Seven Wonders of the Ancient World*, p. 154.

55. Quoted in Clayton and Price, *The Seven Wonders of the Ancient World*, p. 154.

56. Josephus, *Jewish Wars*, p. 282.

57. Clayton and Price, *The Seven Wonders of the Ancient World*, pp. 164–65.

Chronology

B.C.

ca. 5500–3100

The years of Egypt's so-called Predynastic Period, during which the country is divided into many small city-states and eventually into two major kingdoms—Upper Egypt and Lower Egypt.

ca. 3100

A powerful ruler named Menes (or Narmer) unites Upper and Lower Egypt, creating the world's first true nation.

ca. 3100–2686

The years of the Early Dynastic Period, encompassing the reigns of the nine rulers of the First Dynasty and seven rulers of the Second Dynasty.

ca. 2686–2181

The years of the Old Kingdom (encompassing the rulers of the Third, Fourth, Fifth, and Sixth Dynasties), during which most of Egypt's pyramids are built, including the largest ones at Giza (near modern Cairo).

ca. 2589–2566

The reign of the pharaoh Khufu (whom the Greeks called Cheops), who erects the largest of all the pyramids for his tomb.

ca. 2181–2055

The years of the First Intermediate Period, which witnessed much civil strife and a partial breakdown of central authority and law and order.

ca. 2055–1650

The years of the Middle Kingdom (encompassing the Eleventh, Twelfth, Thirteenth, and Fourteenth Dynasties), in which the Egyptians begin expanding their territory by conquest and their wealth through trade.

ca. 1650–1550

The years of the Second Intermediate Period, also called the "Hyksos" period in reference to an Asiatic people of that name who invaded and occupied Egypt.

ca. 1550–1069

The years of the New Kingdom (encompassing the Eighteenth, Nineteenth, and Twentieth Dynasties), in which a series of vigorous pharaohs create an Egyptian empire and erect numerous large temples, palaces, and forts.

ca. 1479–1425

The reign of the pharaoh Thutmose III, who oversees the empire at its largest extent.

ca. 1390–1352

The reign of Amenhotep III, one of Egypt's greatest builder-pharaohs.

ca. 1352–1336

The reign of the pharaoh Amenhotep IV, who took the name Akhenaten; initiated worship of a single god, Aten; and built a new capital city, now referred to as Amarna.

ca. 1279–1213
The reign of Ramesses II, another great builder, who constructs the great rock-hewn temples and giant statues at Abu Simbel.

ca. 1184–1153
The reign of Ramesses III, who defeats the Sea Peoples and builds the fortresslike temple of Medinet Habu.

ca. 1069–747
The years of the Third Intermediate Period, in which Egypt falls into steady military, political, and cultural decline.

ca. 747–332
The years of the Late Period, during most of which members of foreign-born dynasties rule Egypt.

332
The Macedonian Greek conqueror Alexander III (later called "the Great") takes charge of Egypt. The following year he establishes the city of Alexandria, which soon becomes one of the great cities of the ancient world.

323
Alexander dies and his leading generals begin fighting among themselves for possession of his huge empire, which includes most of the Near East, including Egypt. One of these men, Ptolemy, makes himself pharaoh of Egypt, beginning a new royal line, the Ptolemaic dynasty.

323–31
The years of the Ptolemaic Period (or Egypt's Greek Period), during which Ptolemy and his descendants rule Egypt.

31
Cleopatra VII, last of the Ptolemies and the last pharaoh and independent ruler of Egypt, is defeated by the Romans at Actium, Greece. The following year she commits suicide, and Rome makes Egypt a province in its own empire.

30 B.C.–A.D. 395
The years of the Roman Period, in which a series of Roman emperors control Egypt.

A.D.
810
An Arab caliph attempts to tunnel his way into Khufu's great pyramid at Giza to find a great treasure rumored to lie within.

1166
An Arab traveler visits the great lighthouse at Alexandria and later produces a detailed written description.

1303
The great Alexandrian lighthouse topples during a large earthquake.

1798
The French conqueror Napoléon invades Egypt. He brings along more than a hundred scholars to study the country's ancient monuments.

1923
American film director Cecil B. DeMille reproduces a number of ancient Egyptian monuments for his first version of *The Ten Commandments*. He builds even bigger versions for his 1956 remake.

1960s
Threatened by a rising lake, the great temples created by Ramesses II at Abu Simbel are dismantled and reassembled on higher ground.

1990s
Archaeologists discover a workers' village and cemetery near the great pyramids on the Giza plateau.

Glossary

archaeology: The study of past civilizations and their artifacts.

benben: In Egyptian mythology, the primeval (very ancient) mound of creation and first dry land in the world; or a sacred stone representation of the mound.

bronze: A metal alloy made by mixing copper and tin.

casing stones: The smooth limestone blocks forming the outside surfaces of pyramids and some other structures.

colonnade: A row of columns.

colossi (singular is **colossus**): Giant statues.

corbelling: A technique of making roofs (or ceilings) in which layers of stone are stacked so that each layer slightly overhangs the one below it.

crenellation: The notched effect in the battlements of forts, castles, and other ancient and medieval structures.

cult temple: A temple used primarily for standard worship of a god or gods.

dolerite: A very hard type of stone often used by the ancient Egyptians to make stone tools.

dress: To smooth and refine the surface of a block, wall, statue, or other stone object.

dynasty: A line of rulers belonging to a single family.

Egyptology: The branch of archaeology dealing specifically with ancient Egypt.

host: An army unit made up of five hundred soldiers.

hypostyle hall: A large interior chamber whose roof is held up by numerous columns evenly distributed across the room.

inscriptions: Letters and words carved into stone or some other durable material.

mastaba: A low, rectangular tomb made of mud bricks or stone.

mortuary temple: A temple built mainly to maintain a deceased pharoah's spirit and ensure its continued connection to the gods.

nemes: A pleated headdress, covering the top of the forehead and flaring at the sides, that was commonly worn in ancient Egypt.

obelisk: A tall, narrow, pointed stone spire that stood (usually in pairs) near the gates of Egyptian temples.

pylon: A large, flat-topped ceremonial gateway that became a common feature of Egyptian temples, particularly in the New Kingdom.

pyramidion: A pyramid-shaped capstone, usually plated with metal to reflect the sun's rays.

sap: A tunnel dug beneath the walls of a besieged castle, fortress, or city.

sledge: A sledlike device on which ancient workers carried large stones and statues.

sphinx: In ancient Egypt, a mythical creature combining the features or traits of a human and an animal, most often a lion; or a statue representing such a creature.

stele (plural is **stelae**): A stone or wooden marker, often inscribed with text, pictures, or both.

vizier: A pharaoh's chief administrator.

zaa: A group of two hundred Egyptian workers; five *zaa* formed a gang. The Greek word for *zaa* was *phyles.*

For Further Reading

Books

Judith Crosher, *Technology in the Time of Ancient Egypt*. New York: Raintree, 1998. A general look at the building tools and laborsaving devices available to the ancient Egyptians.

George Hart, *Ancient Egypt*. New York: Time-Life, 1995. A very colorfully illustrated introduction to the wonders of ancient Egypt for young readers.

Tim McNeese, *The Pyramids of Giza*. San Diego: Lucent, 1997. This well-written volume explains in considerable detail why and how the Egyptian pyramids were built as well as who built them.

Anne Millard, *Mysteries of the Pyramids*. Brookfield, CT: Copper Beach, 1995. Aimed at basic readers, this book by a noted scholar is short but brightly illustrated and filled with interesting facts about the pyramids and ancient Egyptian life.

Jane Shuter, *Builders and Craftsmen of Ancient Egypt*. Crystal Lake, IL: Heinemann Library, 1998. A well-written general examination of ancient Egyptian builders and artisans.

———, *Life in an Egyptian Workers' Village*. Crystal Lake, IL: Heinemann Library, 2004. Examines what life was like in the residential areas that were erected near the major construction sites in ancient Egypt.

Kelly Trumble, *Cat Mummies*. Boston: Houghton Mifflin, 1999. An unusual and nicely illustrated volume that tells why cats were important in ancient Egyptian society and how these animals were mummified.

Web Sites

Ancient Egyptian Architecture (www. greatbuildings.com/types/styles/ egyptian.html). This site provides links to separate sites, each of which describes an important ancient Egyptian structure. Included are the Great Pyramid of Khufu, Hatshepsut's Temple, the temples at Karnak, and several others.

Building in Ancient Egypt (www.resha fim.org.il/ad/egypt/building). This site discusses the basic building materials and techniques used in ancient Egypt. It also provides links to a wide range of other topics relating to life and work in ancient Egypt.

The Pyramids: The Inside Story (www. pbs.org/wgbh/nova/pyramid). A very informative and entertaining resource sponsored by the prestigious television science program *Nova,* including information on Egyptologist Mark Lehner and his groundbreaking studies and experiments related to ancient Egyptian construction.

Works Consulted

Major Works

Dieter Arnold, *Building in Egypt: Pharaonic Stone Masonry.* Oxford, UK: Oxford University Press, 1991. A thorough, well-illustrated, scholarly overview of Egyptian building methods.

Peter Clayton and Martin Price, *The Seven Wonders of the Ancient World.* New York: Barnes and Noble, 1993. One of the best general studies of these famous monuments, with many insights into the pyramids and the Alexandrian lighthouse.

I.E.S. Edwards, *The Pyramids of Egypt.* New York: Penguin, 1993. One of the classic works about the pyramids by one of the leading Egyptologists of the twentieth century.

Ahmed Fakhry, *The Pyramids.* Chicago: University of Chicago Press, 1961. A good overview of the subject, with several helpful photos and drawings.

Zahi A. Hawass, *The Mysteries of Abu Simbel: Ramesses II and the Temples of the Rising Sun.* Cairo: American University in Cairo Press, 2001. Egypt's greatest archaeologist delivers a fascinating synopsis of the temples and statues at one of the country's major ancient sites.

———, *The Pyramids of Ancient Egypt.* Pittsburgh: Carnegie Museum of Natural History, 1990. A readable overview by one of the leading experts in the field.

Kevin Jackson and Jonathan Stamp, *Building the Great Pyramid.* Toronto: Firefly, 2003. This nicely organized account of the planning and construction methods of the builders is supported by many color photos and drawings.

Mark Lehner, *The Complete Pyramids.* London: Thames and Hudson, 1997. A superior treatment of the subject, strengthened by data from Lehner's famous experiments re-creating ancient Egyptian construction techniques.

George Reisner, *The Development of the Egyptian Tomb Down to the Accession of Cheops.* Brockton, MA: Pye Rare, 1996. An excellent overview of Egyptian tombs, from the first mastabas to the Valley of the Kings and beyond.

Gay Robins, *Egyptian Statues.* Buckinghamshire, UK: Shire, 2003. This work ably discusses the styles, functions, and making of statues, including giant ones like the Sphinx and the colossi of Ramesses II.

David P. Silverman, ed., *Ancient Egypt.* New York: Oxford University Press, 1997. A very useful general depiction of ancient Egyptian culture, with a large section on architecture and building.

Steven Snape, *Egyptian Temples.* Buckinghamshire, UK: Shire, 1999. Well illustrated, this is a good general introduction that discusses cult temples, mortuary temples, and atypical temples like those at Abu Simbel.

Desmond Stewart, *The Pyramids and the Sphinx.* New York: Newsweek Book Division, 1971. A readable synopsis of the major ancient Egyptian monuments, including an entire chapter on the Sphinx at Giza.

Nigel and Helen Strudwick, *Thebes in Egypt: A Guide to the Tombs and Temples of Ancient Luxor.* Ithaca, NY: Cornell University Press, 1999. One of the best available general studies of the temple complexes in the region of ancient Thebes.

Richard H. Wilkinson, *The Complete Temples of Ancient Egypt.* London: Thames and Hudson, 2000. Similar to Snape's book (see above), but more comprehensive and more detailed.

Other Important Works

Primary Sources

J.H. Breasted, ed., *Ancient Records of Egypt.* Vols. 1 and 2. New York: Russell and Russell, 1962.

Diodorus Siculus, *Library of History.* 12 vols. Cambridge, MA: Harvard University Press, 1962–67.

Herodotus, *The Histories.* Trans. Aubrey de Sélincourt. New York: Penguin, 1972.

Homer, *Odyssey.* Trans. E.V. Rieu. Baltimore: Penguin, 1961.

Josephus, *The Jewish Wars.* Trans. G.A. Williamson. Rev. E. Mary Smallwood. New York: Penguin, 1981.

Miriam Lichtheim, ed., *Ancient Egyptian Literature: A Book of Readings.* 2 vols. Berkeley and Los Angeles: University of California Press, 1975–76.

Josephine Mayer and Tom Prideaux, eds., *Never to Die: The Egyptians in Their Own Words.* New York: Viking, 1938.

Pliny the Elder, *Natural History,* in *Natural History: A Selection.* Trans. John F. Healy. New York: Penguin, 1991.

Plutarch, *Life of Alexander,* in *The Age of Alexander: Nine Greek Lives by Plutarch.* Trans. Ian Scott-Kilvert. New York: Penguin, 1973.

James B. Pritchard, ed., *Ancient Near Eastern Texts Relating to the Old Testament.* Princeton, NJ: Princeton University Press, 1969.

W.K. Simpson, ed., *The Literature of Ancient Egypt: An Anthology of Stories, Instructions, and Poetry.* New Haven, CT: Yale University Press, 1973.

Strabo, *Geography.* Vol. 8. Trans. Horace L. Jones. Cambridge, MA: Harvard University Press, 1964.

Modern Sources

Paul G. Bahn, ed., *The Cambridge Illustrated History of Archaeology.* New York: Cambridge University Press, 1996.

Bob Brier, *Ancient Egyptian Magic.* New York: HarperCollins, 2001.

Lionel Casson, *Ancient Egypt.* New York: Time-Life, 1965.

———, *Daily Life in Ancient Egypt.* New York: American Heritage, 1975.

Somers Clarke and R. Engelbach, *Ancient Egyptian Construction and Architecture.* New York: Dover, 1990.

Peter Connolly, *Greece and Rome at War.* London: Greenhill, 1998.

Fabio Bourbon, *Egypt: Yesterday and Today. Lithographs and Diaries by Daniel Roberts.*

Shrewsbury, UK: Stuart, Tabor, and Chang, 1996.

Nicolas Grimal, *A History of Ancient Egypt.* Trans. Ian Shaw. Oxford, UK: Blackwell, 1992.

Zahi Hawass, "Tombs of the Pyramid Builders," *Archaeology,* January/February 1997.

———, "The Discovery of the Tombs of the Pyramid Builders." www.guardians.net/hawass/buildtomb.htm.

Zahi Hawass and Mark Lehner, "Builders of the Pyramids," *Archaeology,* January/February 1997.

Alfred Lucas and J.R. Harris, *Ancient Egyptian Materials and Industries.* Mineola, NY: Dover, 1999.

Nicholas Reeves, *Ancient Egypt: The Great Discoveries.* New York: Thames and Hudson, 2000.

Manuel Robbins, *The Collapse of the Bronze Age: The Story of Greece, Troy, Israel, Egypt, and the Peoples of the Sea.* San Jose, CA: Authors Choice, 2001.

Chris Scarre, ed., *The Seventy Wonders of the Ancient World.* London: Thames and Hudson, 1999.

George Bernard Shaw, *Caesar and Cleopatra.* Baltimore: Penguin, 1966.

Ian Shaw, *Egyptian Warfare and Weapons.* Buckinghamshire, UK: Shire, 1991.

Ian Shaw and Paul Nicholson, *The Dictionary of Ancient Egypt.* New York: Harry N. Abrams, 1995.

William S. Smith, *The Art and Architecture of Ancient Egypt.* New York: Penguin, 1965.

Eugen Strouhal, *Life of the Ancient Egyptians.* Norman: University of Oklahoma Press, 1992.

Philip J. Watson, *Pyramids and Mastaba Tombs of the Old and Middle Kingdoms.* Princes Risborough, UK: Shire, 1987.

Yigael Yadin, *The Art of Warfare in Biblical Lands in the Light of Archaeological Study.* Vol. 1. New York: McGraw-Hill, 1963.

Index

Picture Credits

About the Author

Historian and award-winning writer Don Nardo has written or edited numerous books
about the ancient world, including *Empires of Mesopotamia, The Ancient Greeks, Life of
a Roman Gladiator, The Etruscans, Ancient Civilizations,* and the *Greenhaven Encyclopedia
of Greek and Roman Mythology.* Mr. Nardo lives with his wife, Christine, in Massachusetts.